Bigfoot Chronicles
True Encounters with The Legend known as Bigfoot.
Book 1

By Melissa George

Cover Illustration Copyright © 2020 by Melissa George
Cover design by Melissa George
Book design and production by Melissa George
Cover Images from Morgue File, or personal images.

Research for Authenticity, Cari George, Marty George, Chris George

Names and places have been changed to protect people and properties. This story has been vetted for truth and authenticity.

Before you begin, please let me remind you that I am an Independent Author. My books are created by me. They are all written in General Casual. If you find the occasional Typo. I apologize. I don't have a group of people sitting in their office waiting to go over my book before it reaches you. The English used in the majority of my books may not be proper at times. This is better to convey the story to you just as it was told to me without sounding like a textbook. With this being said. I hope you enjoy this book cover to cover. If you do, please think about leaving me a review. Your reviews can make or break an independent author. If you didn't care for the book. I understand. We can't connect with every book. Just try to go easy on me with your review. Thank you.

This book is dedicated to the members of our team,

The Carolina Cryptid Crew.

Thank you for believing and trusting.

Keep seeking the Truth, while hunting the Legends.

If you had told me three years ago that, I would be writing this book, I would have laughed at you. Now, I do not find the subject funny at all. Sometimes, I find it a bit scary and intimidating.

Since the beginning of this book, I have done more in-depth research on the subject. I have read that some believe Bigfoot ties in with the paranormal phenomenon. I cannot say if this is true or not, but I can say I have had my fair share of both. These experiences have taught me a lot and changed me in some profound ways. I am a much more open-minded person. I have always heard that "seeing is believing," and I pretty much lived by this. However, I can honestly say now; that is not true. Your heart will always know the truth way before your mind has ever accepted it. Over the years, I have discovered that our heart is open to believing things that our eyes and brain will deny.

Now I am going to give you my experiences and let you draw your own conclusions. I am a real person just like you. Look me up on Facebook. The only difference between you and me is, I have had a few experiences in my life that maybe you have yet to have.

Names and events portrayed in this book are accurate and true; any locations have been changed to protect the people that live there.

For the Bigfoot enthusiasts out there, you will probably see the signs long before we ever did. It took my mind a while to catch up with my heart.

For you skeptics out there, it is perfectly fine if you don't believe a word of this, I was there myself at one time. Maybe you can just look at this book as a work of fiction and enjoy reading.

If you are looking for that experience, I can only hope that one day you find it and join us "believers."

I am a skeptical girl. I have to have that, "In your face" experience, for me to know it is real. Now...... I know... IT IS REAL.

I am going to start you out in the beginning, long before we realized that the land held a big secret.

I was born in a small town in rural North West, South Carolina. The locals call this area, the "Upstate." Actually, "The Upstate" is a small cluster of individual towns. Each of them still contains a lot of farming land and many wooded areas. I grew up here, right next door to my grandfather's farm.

It was my mom's dad; we called him Pa Beatty. He was a tall, slim man that worked hard but always had time for his grandchildren. He and I would go for walks around his large yard in the evenings. I remember him picking a pear from the pear tree for me and peeling it with his pocketknife. He would peel it completely, leaving a single spiral. I found this to be amazing. I still cannot do it! However, just as the sun started to drop down in the sky, he would tell me it was time to go home. He would then walk me out to the front yard where he could watch me walk to my house. Every time I reach my front door, I would look back and see Pa Beatty turn and walk toward his own front door. Did he know something back then that the rest of us did not?

My father bought the land that we lived on now when I was around thirteen. It was just a few miles from where I had grown up on my grandfather's farm. The land was uncleared; there were acres upon acres of trees and dense vegetation. The first time I ever saw the property, I wondered how in the world we would ever get such land cleared enough for a home.

However, my father did it. I think he had made it his mission to have his own land for us to call home. We actually got the land cleared and moved here when I was about sixteen. My grandfather had suffered a few strokes by this time, so my parents moved him beside us.

We were the only people on this little country road. There was nothing around but woods, a creek, and the swamp. For the first time in my life, I refused to stay home alone after dark. The place had a creepy feel to it, and I always had the feeling of being watched.

My father had purchased many acres here, so it was to be home for a long time to come.

Growing up, I had always enjoyed getting out and walking in the woods, playing in the creeks, and just enjoying nature. Sometimes I would take a book or my homework from school, find myself a big tree, and just sit. I loved hearing the wind in the leaves, the smell of the earth. I liked the solitude and the quiet. I loved watching all the small animals. They would be curious as to why I was there. Some would even get curious and come close to me.

As much as I loved the woods, I was never comfortable in our new place. There was just something about it that made me feel on edge. I assumed it was because we were so far away from other people. The nearest neighbors lived about half a mile from us.

When my friends would come over, we would walk through the woods, and even they too felt like we were being watched. It was just a strange feeling that kept you looking over your shoulder. I was constantly looking up from my book and scanning the trees, hoping to catch a glimpse of whom or what was watching me. I never saw anything.

One night after hanging out with friends, I drove down our driveway and parked the car.

Instead of going inside, I walked over to the swing in the side yard. It was around midnight, and the stars were bright.

I sat there on the swing watching the stars and listening to the night sounds. Suddenly I felt eyes on me. My back was to the woods, and that unnerved me. Just as I was about to stand up and go inside, I heard a heavy breath. It was a deep throaty breath and seemed to come from just over my left shoulder. A bolt of terror shot through my body, and my danger alarm kicked in. I stood up and quickly walked to my front door, not looking back. It felt like I was in slow motion trying to get my key in the front door lock. I got the door opened and stepped inside, making sure to lock the door behind me. I felt instant relief. I was safe now; my parents were both in bed asleep. But would come running if I needed them. I went to my room and started getting ready for bed. I kept thinking about that loud breath I had heard. What could that have been? It didn't sound human. Now I am wondering what kind of animal could make that sound. It would have to be something big.

I walked over to the window and barely pulled the curtains back just enough to see out in case there was something or someone still out there. I could see across the yard to the tree line. The outside light cast strange shadows in the yard. In the dim light, just by the swing, I could barely make out a figure. It did not move there in the dark. Maybe my mom had planted another tree there. I had been gone all day, and she was still decorating the yard with flowers, trees, and shrubs. What I was looking at had to be a tree; it was too tall to be an animal or a man. After convincing myself that there was nothing out there, I watched this tree crouch down! A bolt of terror shot through my body!

There was a bear in our yard! That did it for me; I grabbed my pillow and headed for the couch in the living room, which put me closer to my sleeping parents.

The next morning I told my dad what I had seen. He said that it could have been a bear, but it was highly unlikely. Bears are hardly ever seen in our area.

Mom was convinced that I just saw strange shadows, as we had not lived here very long. I cannot say for sure what I saw.

I was always unnerved now when I would come home late at night. My inner self-knew there was something in those woods, and whatever it was could be dangerous.

I had lived here for about a year when I met my husband, Marty. Like me, he, too, had grown up in South Carolina. We met at high school, became best friends, and were soon married. Within a year, we had a baby boy, Chris. We moved a few times during our first few years. We lived in town for the most part; I found out very quickly that I was not a city person. How do these people sleep at night? The sounds of car doors slamming, people talking, sirens and train whistles were just too much for me. I was ready to find a place in the country. When our son turned three, we moved back onto my family's property.

My grandfather had passed away, and my parents lived on the property by themselves now. Therefore, we bought my grandfather's home, and we were here to stay. It was the perfect place to raise our son. He had all the woods and creeks to explore and play in. These woods would be the perfect place for Chris and all of his friends.

As Chris got older, he and his friends spent countless hours behind our house in the woods; on any given day, our front yard got littered with boys bicycles, yet you hardly ever saw any of them. They were out in the woods, climbing trees, building forts and catching crayfish in the creek. I was thrilled to have my son grow up this way. I felt in my heart that these woods were just meant for little boys to explore them.

Chris and a few of his friends came into the house late one-afternoon, swearing they had seen a bear. I was cooking dinner in the kitchen, and I could overhear them telling Marty what they had seen. They had been catching baby turtles near the swamp when they heard something grunting. They stopped playing and looked around the woods. The sound had stopped, so they went back to playing. They soon heard a loud rustling in the leaves; the grunting began again, and it was closer this time. They looked around, and one of the older boys saw its face look around a tree at them. He screamed, "Bear!" They all took off running for the house. They had been quite a ways down in the woods, so as they were telling their story, their words were coming in breathy gasps.

I snickered to myself, thinking they had just spooked one another.

Bears are uncommon here. Marty just told them to stay away from the swamp for a while. Not to be that far in the woods.

The next Saturday, Marty wanted to check out the woods just to make sure things were safe for the kids. I was up for a hike, so I tagged along with the guys. While walking, we came across what looked to be an old home place. As we trudged single file through the trees, we came out into a large clearing. You could plainly tell that this area had been someone's yard many years ago. The grass had grown tall, but there was no thick underbrush like there had been in the woods. There were a rose bush and some azaleas that had been taken over with vines. Daffodils were arranged around two large oak trees.

An old, dilapidated barn stood covered in vines and kudzu. Looking at it from the outside, it looked like it would collapse in on itself with just the slightest breeze. The rusty tin roof barely showed through the thick vines. However, walking inside was a different story. The wood still looked new! As we entered, I could smell the hay and cattle. The gates still swung on shiny hooks.

The cattle shoot sat open, waiting for the cows to be loaded. I could not believe what I was looking at! No vines or weeds had grown inside at all. It looked as if the farmer had just gone home for lunch. Amazed, I was examining the wood when I came across some cow bones. They, too, looked well preserved. However, for some reason, they made me very uneasy. I was ready to leave once I saw them. I called Marty and Chris over to look at what I had just found. We all speculated on what animal could have taken down a cow. There is no way A cow could have wandered in here and gotten stuck. The entry was very wide and very distinct. The only way it could not have gotten out is if it were trapped in here by another animal or if it was killed and brought in here. Also, whatever had it, had eaten it in one of the stalls. Not out in the open floor. That is not something a coyote would do. Either way, I felt a chill go up my spine, and I was ready to leave.

As we left the old barn, we warned Chris not to be down here playing around it. It looked as if it could cave in at any time. Chris was perfectly fine with that. He had much rather be playing in the woods and creek anyway.

Our woods contain a creek and huge swamp that eventually leads into Hartwell Lake. Lake Hartwell is a man-made reservoir bordering Georgia and South Carolina on the Savannah, Tugaloo, and Seneca Rivers

We have quite an abundance of wildlife here; we have the wild boar, turkeys, deer, coyotes, red fox, bobcat, opossum, raccoons, an occasional gator, and sometimes a black bear or two. At times, these creatures would enter our back yard. It is nice to sit on the back porch and watch them. We have placed No hunting and no trespassing signs all over the property. The animals have come to see this as their sanctuary. We put out sweet feed for the deer and corn for the turkeys. A little red fox and her babies make a meal out of our table scraps every evening. It has always been a peaceful place to live. It never crossed my mind that we would share this property with these creatures of legend. I cannot say for sure if they live here or migrate through here at certain times of the year. But I can say, without a doubt, they are here, on this land.

I was about nine years old when I first heard the term Bigfoot. One summer evening, in 1976, my older cousin and I sat alone on my grandparent's front porch. Our bare legs dangled over the edge. My cousin lived in town. She and her family would come out on the weekends to visit our grandparents. I lived right next door, so she and I would hang out together. It was getting late, and I was thinking about walking home when we heard this horrible scream.

My Grandfather had a huge farm that was surrounded by woods. This scream had come from the woods on the backside of the property. I was sure this sound had come from an animal. However, it was not an animal I was familiar with.

My Grandfather was the all-American farmer. There were Cows, horses, pigs, chickens, dogs, and tons of cats. Every spring, he would get on his tractor and plant two enormous gardens. He grew one for the family, the other to sell. There is just no way to guess how many acres he had. It seemed as if this farm went on forever. The yard around the house was just massive. I can remember it taking my father all day to cut the grass. Where the yard ended, the woods began.

Woods on all three sides surrounded the property. Sometimes we would walk through the woods to get to the creek. In the summer, my cousins and I would find a spot where the beavers had dammed it up, and we would spend all day playing in the water.

"Was that one of the hogs?" I asked.

The direction this scream came from contained a big cow pasture and the pig lots.

"No, I don't think so." She said. "It may have been a Bigfoot."

"What?" I asked.

She then told me about a big hairy monster that lived in the woods. He would eat Papa's pigs and chickens if he could get them. She warned me to be careful when feeding the dogs and the pigs. If he smelled the food, he would come after me! I am sure my eyes were the size of saucers. I was thinking of feeding the hogs. My mom would often give me the table scraps from dinner and have me go dump it in the pig lot. Naturally, the pigs were a good way from the house. Most evenings, just before sunset, I would walk across the backyard to a small footpath in the underbrush.

The weeds and grass grew wild here at the edge of the yard. This path wound in between a few sparse trees with the brush being head high in places.

It opened into a clearing. This clearing is where the pig lots were. There were two stalls with roofs on them inside a huge fence. On the left side of the lot, my dad would keep the ground wet for the pigs to roll in the mud. Luckily, I did not have to enter the fence to pour out my bucket; the trough was placed against the fence near the gate, so I lifted my bucket and poured it over the fence.

Sometimes my brother and I would come down here and play with the baby piglets. If we ever made one of them squeal, mama pig would be after us like a mad hornet. She would come barreling out of her stall snorting and grunting! She sounded like a freight train coming after us! It didn't take us, but a few seconds to drop that piglet and climb the fence! We would sit on top and wait for her to calm down and return to her stall, then we would do it all over again.

The sun was always low in the sky by the time I made it back into our yard and casting long creepy shadows.

Now I dreaded having to do this, knowing there was something out there waiting and watching! She was my older cousin, and I truly believed her.

I sat there a while longer, not looking forward to the walk home by myself and really wishing that I had gone home while it was still light out. I had stayed too late; I was sure Pa Beatty was already settled in for the night. He would not be there to watch me walk home. I was thinking about the monster. Maybe since I did not have any food, the monster wouldn't come after me...

I did walk home by myself. I did not want to look like a baby to my older cousin. However, I heard every little noise. The sounds seemed to be magnified. At one point, I thought I was being followed. Therefore, I sped up to a fast walk, thinking if I ran, it would surely chase me down. My heart was pounding out of my chest. I could hear it in my ears. I did not dare to look behind me; I didn't want to see this monster.

I knew I had probably spooked myself because once I got inside, the fear was gone.

The next day, I asked my mom if there was such a thing as a Bigfoot. She said, "Some people say there is." She did not say no! For me, that set it in stone; in fact, that may have scared me worse than what my cousin had said. As far as I was concerned, they existed. Now I was thinking that I was going to have to be very careful while I was outside, and with it being summer, my life was spent outside. Great! Now I was going to spend the rest of my summer in fear of some big hairy creature that made horrible screams.

This thought hung in my mind the rest of the summer. However, the thought of Bigfoot faded with the season.

As I grew older and heard more about these huge creatures, I realized that my cousin had gotten her facts wrong. For one thing, they usually go after the wildlife instead of farm animals, and there were none even remotely close to our area of the US.

The majority of accounts I had heard of so far were in the extreme northwest, not in our little part of South Carolina. I got interested in the possibility that these things could actually exist. It was both scary and exciting at the same time.

It sounded like something out of a Science Fiction Movie. I was amazed that there were Native Americans that had drawn pictures of these large beasts so many years ago. What had they actually been seeing then, could it have been a bear walking upright? Could it have been some kind of feral human? These explanations were not unlikely.

There seem to be many people all over the world have claimed to have seen one. With so many accounts of sightings, there has to be more to this than just some "Made up monster." There were too many people seeing these creatures or something closely resembling them for them not to exist.

At this time, I had not checked any databases to see how many reports there actually were. I knew that there had to be something more to this.

There is no way these things could go as far back as the early Native Americans seeing them, and many people today seeing them for it to be nothing. However, being that there were none remotely close to where we lived, I didn't dwell on it. I would watch the shows that came on TV, but it would be forgotten as soon as I changed the channel.

Years passed. Chris grew up, as did all the local children. The woods were no longer a playground; in fact, they lay quiet for approximately ten years.

Chris had started a family of his own. He and his wife want to raise their children here on the family property. Therefore, Chris, Cari, and their two children are living with us until they can put their own home here.

A couple of years ago a show called "Finding Big Foot" aired on TV. Of course, with having an interest in this, the show intrigued me. My family and I watched it for entertainment purposes more than anything else.

Then I got interested in the evidence they would find. The witnesses they spoke with seemed sincere to me, not just some paid actors. Watching the show led me to check out their website. I found the BFRO site to be quite extensive.

I began reading about people's encounters. While reading accounts in other states, it occurred to me to check South Carolina just to see if anything was there. I did this purely on a whim. To my surprise, there were two encounters listed! The first one was about fifteen miles away. I was highly intrigued.

As I read the second one, my heart skipped a beat. There was a sighting listed, less than a mile from where we live. If you walked through the woods, it wasn't far away at all. Also, some chicken houses sat right in the center between my house and the sighting. I had read many encounters of possible Bigfoot stealing chickens. However, this could just be a coincidence.

I would love to be able to talk to this person. However, this sighting was over ten years ago.

This person may not even live in the area anymore. Furthermore, there was not any actual proof that the claim was true. It could have just as easily been mistaken identity. There was just no way of knowing. I still showed the page to the family. Chris and Cari had been just as shocked as I had been. Marty, being skeptical, didn't have much to say.

The thought of this person seeing something locally kept playing in my mind for days to come. What did he see? Why was it there? The article said that this thing had been seen in the middle of the road, and it ran off into the woods.

Those woods are connected to our woods. I looked up
the surrounding area on Google Maps. I was shocked
to see just how close this sighting actually was. That
would put this creature almost in our back yard. I had
so many questions, with no answers. If only I could
sit down and talk with this person.

Later on, thanks to the help of my daughter in law, I
did get to speak with this person. We have not met
face to face, but we have spoken on the phone.
He says he will remember this creature for the rest of
his life. He is now an ex-Marine with children and
grandchildren; therefore, I will not disclose his
identity. In speaking with him, I could tell by his tone
and description of the creature that he did, in fact,
see something that was not a bear. It was back in
eighty-four when he saw this thing. That is the same
time that I, as a young teenager, was feeling very
frightened of our woods and saw something in the
shadows. Coincidence? Possibly. That is just one more
of my million unanswered questions.

This image is from Google maps showing the
proximity of our home and the sighting listed on the
BFRO page.

The following is the sighting in his own words, with his permission to use.

For years, our neighbors would tell us that there was a Bigfoot that roamed the woods where we lived. We thought that it was a way to keep us from wandering off and finding the illegal plants they may have been growing. The only reason we somewhat believed them was, the grandmother who told us the same thing was a minister at a local church. She is no longer with us.

The day I saw what I believe to be a Bigfoot was a summer day around 7:45 to 8:30ish. My sister and I were going to visit our friends. She was driving. We travel this route all the time. During the school year, the bus travels this route also. The reason I say this is to let you know, I am familiar with the area. As we approached the small bridge that crosses a pond that we call a swamp, we both noticed it in the middle of the road. At first, I thought it was a bear. As she slowed the car and hit the horn, it stood up, looked in our direction and took off across the swamp.

I have seen many bears, twice too close for comfort. I had one to stand up in front of me in my grandma's backyard. I think it was spooked as much as I was. We both ran. It ran away on four legs. So I know what I saw was not a bear. I remember being amazed by watching this thing run. I asked my sister to turn around and go back. She locked the doors and turned around. When we got back, there was something on the road that it must have been eating. A rabbit, opossum some type of small animal. Probably roadkill. The creature was dark brown at least 6 to 7 feet tall. It happened so quick, I was not able to get a good look at the face.

All I remember was it was big, hairy, large back with no neck. I was 16 years old at the time, my sister was 18. No one believed us. Not even our neighbors. I am now 34.

I can still see the image in my head.

What made me recall this was the footage, where the men on horses record it walking away. Seeing that thing walking back into the woods looking at the large back and the muscle, man!

(This concludes his story.)

I will never know if his sighting and my nighttime encounter were coincidences or even the same creature. I just find it strange that it happened to both of us within such a small proximity.

As I have mentioned before, we have an abundance of wildlife here. Therefore, you get pretty used to the way most of the animals behave. Marty had been sitting outside one evening when he came in to get the camera.

I look up from my computer, "What's up?" I ask, glancing at the camera in his hand.

"There are two beautiful owls out there he says," heading back outside.

No sooner did he go out, then he comes back in.

"Babe, you have got to come out and see this." He says. "You are not going to believe it."

I get up and walk out to our back porch with him.

He was right. The site was unbelievable. There had to be twenty-five owls, sitting just at the tree line of our back yard! They were beautiful. However, I also knew they could be a threat. I had just purchased a Boston Terrier puppy. He would make the perfect meal for one of these Owls. As beautiful as they are, they are also predator birds.

"What would cause them to do this?" I asked

"I have no clue," Marty responds. "I have never seen anything like it. Either they are tracking a food source. Or something in those woods sees them as a food source." He says.
"What kind of animal would do that?" I wondered aloud. Now curious, I had to go look this up. I found out that the Owls would eat insects, small animals, and sometimes other birds. But I could not find anything that would attack an Owl or make them behave this way. How strange! Maybe there were some field mice in the back yard? But would field mice draw this many Owls?

The Owls continued to show up every evening, just at the end of the yard. It was almost as if they did not want to be in the woods. They caused me to have to watch my puppy very closely. At four every evening, I had to make sure he was in the house. I also wondered if they could harm our grandchildren. They finally became a nuisance.

I called our local DNR. They told me I would just have to live with it. It is illegal to kill an Owl. Who knew?

They did not seem to fear us at all. If we sat down in the lower part of our yard in the evenings, they would perch right above our heads. They seemed not to care that we were sitting there.

I have never known any bird behave this way. I was intrigued by them being there, but I was also unnerved with their strange behavior. I did not fancy being attacked by a rabid owl. They can carry rabies. It is unlikely to be attacked by one. Like it is unlikely that they would perch this way in our yard. I started asking friends and neighbors if they had ever experienced such strange behavior. Of course, they looked at me as if I were crazy. Owls just do not behave this way! While I am very well aware of that fact, I still have a back yard full of Owls!

Sitting outside one day pondering our owl invasion, I noticed that there was not a single squirrel in my yard. I could understand if they went into hiding from the Owls in the early evening. For them, not be running across the yard or playing in the trees was highly unusual. We had such an abundance of Squirrels that they had actually become a nuisance. They would jump from the trees and land on our house with a thud. Then you could hear their little feet scurrying across the roof. My dogs hated it when they did this. Therefore, they would try to threaten the squirrels with the loudest barks possible!
This made me dislike the squirrels on the roof as well. At one point, a couple of the Squirrels had decided they liked the taste of our shingles! So saying they were a problem was an understatement. But where did they all go, and why?

Luckily, Turkey season started not long after. We could hear the hunters shooting from the neighboring fields. I am assuming the sounds of the guns scared the Owls away.

I was just happy that the owls had left. My puppy and grandchildren were safe to play outside again. I never did figure out why they came out of the woods the way they did. They seemed to leave just as mysteriously.

Every year the Wild Turkeys were fun to watch. We would hear them clucking long before they ever came into sight. Late in the afternoon, they would come from a nearby field and cross over into our yard. They would walk the side of our yard and slip into the woods.

There were easily fifteen birds in this flock. There were a few big males, some hens, and a ton of little chicks. I never got to count them to know for sure how many were there. But each year, the little flock got bigger. Every evening, just like clockwork, we had the turkey parade.

Each year, Marty and Chris would get us one for our freezer. We usually cooked it when we could have the whole family together. It is always fun to roast a big game bird in the summer.

That is the only thing that has ever been shot on our property. As much as I love Venison, when I get it, either I purchase it, or a friend gives us some. The deer have a haven here. It has always been that way.

Chris and Marty post up just at the edge of the yard. When the Turkey parade starts, they wait for a huge gobbler. BAM! From inside the house, I hear one single shot. I know it will take them a little while to get him cleaned up and ready for the freezer. I just go about what I'm doing and never give it another thought. After a while, Marty and Chris come in.

"Is he in the freezer?" I ask.
 I am assuming they had put the bird in the freezer on our back porch.

"Not exactly." Says Chris.

Knowing this was not a normal response, I guess now they must have missed him. But there are so many of them, why didn't they fire again?

"So." "What happened?" I asked.

Marty says, "We shot him." "The blast knocked him up into the air, and then he landed in a small ravine just inside the tree line. We went to get him, and he was gone."

"Gone?" I ask. "How?"

"It is as if he just disappeared." Marty said."There were a few feathers and some blood where we hit him. Then nothing."

They had walked the woods looking for the injured turkey. They even checked up in the trees. It was as if it just vanished! They were both clearly confused as to how this big bird just disappeared.

Two days later, my Dad and Chris had the same thing happen to them. They shot the turkey, and it just disappeared. They, too, went to look for the missing bird, but it had just vanished. My dad said it was the strangest thing he had ever encountered. He said that it being gone was not uncommon, it was them not being able to find it that confused him. They saw it was hit, yet when they went to retrieve their bird, it was gone. They searched the woods for an hour looking for this bird, but it was never found.

Marty and Chris waited about a week and tried again with the same results. That makes three injured if not dead, turkeys that have just vanished! We finally gave up one having our turkey. It would be senseless to kill any more of them when we had already lost three.

None of us had an explanation for this. Like most things that you can't find a valid answer for, they just get pushed to the back of your mind until something happens, which causes you to recall it.

Now I think I may know just where our turkeys went.

Not long after this, our closest neighbor, "Tom," came walking down our driveway. Marty happened to be out in the yard, so he greeted him with a handshake.

I was in the kitchen finishing the dishes, I dried my hands on a towel and went out to see what was up. It was odd to have Tom walk so far when most of the time, he drove down to our house. As I walked out, he was in the middle of telling Marty that he was looking for his two small dogs.

He said that they were kept inside, but he had let them out for a potty break, and they had both ran to the top of his driveway barking. His driveway is roughly ten feet from his front door. Then maybe ten yards to the top of his driveway from there it slopes down to the highway. He said they ran to the top of the driveway, then disappeared from sight as they ran down the short slope to the road. He was right behind them, so they were only out of sight for about one minute. By the time he got to the top of his driveway where he could see down, they were gone. He heard nothing at all. He could only assume someone had picked them up, yet when we asked him, he stated that he had not seen or heard a car. Also, it was very unlikely that anyone around here would stop and pick up two small dogs wearing collars. Most of the time, if anyone spots a wandering dog, we try to find out whom it belongs to and return it to the owner. This just did not make any sense to us. How did his dogs go missing that fast? His driveway borders our woods. All one would have to do is cross the road to enter our woods. We told him we would keep an eye out for his dogs, and if we found them, we would call him. After he had left, Marty and I walked back into the house.

"I just hate that he has lost his dogs," I said.

Marty said, "yeah," "especially after his other one went missing last year."

"Oh, no!" I exclaimed. "You're right!".
However, it was a bigger dog. I now remembered us seeing Tom driving slowly up and down our road one evening. He finally drove down the driveway to ask if we had seen his dog. It was the same scenario. He had let the dog out to use the bathroom. It ran across the yard barking and just disappeared down the driveway. To my knowledge, it was never found. Now that I look back, all the dogs went missing around four-thirty to five o clock. Strange. We never did find his two dogs. He did not either.

I was working on my computer, setting up a website for a new client. This is long and tedious work; sometimes, a job could last for days. I reach out for my coffee cup. Empty. I was going to have to get up and make a pot. I wasn't sure just how much I had drunk over the past few hours.

However, I was sure the pot would have to be empty. My daughter in law and I both work from home. Between the two of us, we could easily drain a coffee pot. I went to stand up; the pain shot up my back and legs! Boy, I had been sitting there a while. I had gotten stiff from not moving for so long. I go to put on the coffee and notice the timer on the coffee pot. I had already put in a good six hours. It was time for a well-needed break! I figured I would enjoy a fresh cup of coffee and do a bit of research on things I would eventually need for this client. As I was scrolling along, I came across a Bigfoot article. Along with the article was a YouTube video. Therefore, I click over and watch.

After watching this video, I see there are about ten more on the right side of my screen. I had just acquired my new found love! I had hundreds of Bigfoot videos to entertain me for hours on end!

I found myself relaxing with a few of these videos every evening. Also, I was actually learning quite a bit from other people's experiences. I was amazed at just how many "normal" people had encounters with these large beasts. While I watched these videos, my husband and daughter in law would listen to them.

We all enjoyed hearing about the different encounters. How each one was different, yet they all had some common factors. I started to put some things together with the encounters other people were having. Some people seemed to think they were somehow linked to the paranormal. I have no idea if this holds true or not. However, I do know that my family has had some paranormal encounters.

This began to be a regular evening event. I would turn the volume up and watch the videos as they listened. This is where we first learned of rock clacks, tree knocks, whoops, yells, and tree structures. I never knew that these videos would play a big part in my life in the months ahead.

As we all know, with Turkey season comes planting season. So I had sent Marty and Chris out to the lower part of the woods to get some wild English Ivy for me. It had to be late February or March, as I like to plant my Ivy about the same time as planting season.

This Ivy grows in the deepest part of the woods, Not too far from the swamp. It makes wonderful hanging baskets for the summer. When the guys got home that day, they had quite a story to tell. While they were digging up the Ivy, Marty had looked up for a moment. He noticed there was mud all over the nearby trees. He said at; first, it appeared as if a bear had shaken the mud from his coat after coming out of the swamp. He and Chris walked over to take a better look and noticed that the mud was on top of the leaves, with none underneath them. They ended up following the mud out of the woods into the open area of the old barn with waist-high grass. The grass had been packed down in this area as if something large had moved through that was covered in mud.

They followed this packed down grass back into the woods. There they saw that the mud was over seven feet high. Chris is an easy six foot two. He said he reached up as high as he could and pulled some branches down. This is when they noticed the mud on the upper leaves, looked like brush strokes. Therefore, they knew it was something with fur. How could that possibly be a bear? It was excessively high. Could this have been where a bear had stood up, and the leaves brushed the top of its head?

No, it looked more as if the leaves had brushed along the legs or torso. But they were much too high for this. Bears do not walk on two feet. Marty told us not to be near the woods; there had to be a large bear somewhere nearby. For the next little while, we did keep our eye out for a rogue bear. We never saw anything. And it was eventually forgotten. Now when I look back on that day, I find it rather scary. I will always wonder just how close they came to the big guy, without even knowing they had been following a Bigfoot.

Not long after this, Marty and I woke in the middle of the night to a blood- curdling scream! We both sat straight up in bed. This was a horrible scream. My heart was pounding in my chest!

We assumed two of our Pit Bulls were fighting. Marty and I both race out the front door, thinking we were going to have to get out there quick to separate two dogs. I was wondering which one had escaped their kennel and praying it wasn't Kandie, she was the most aggressive of all the dogs if she was fighting, the other dog was going to be hurt badly. By the time we reach the front door, the night was dead silent. We both stopped to listen.

There was no noise at all. The crickets and bullfrogs were even silent. How odd. Being that we raised Pit Bulldogs for many years, we knew this could not have been a dogfight. Their fights do not end so abruptly. What in the world made that noise? Still being a bit confused as to what had just happened, we both turn and head back to bed. I lay there for a while wondering just what kind of creature in the woods could make such a noise, A Bobcat, A Panther? I soon fell back into an uneasy sleep.

Over coffee the next morning, I asked Chris and Cari if they had heard anything. They both said they had slept soundly through the night. I still wondered just what had woken us up. That scream was unlike anything I had ever heard before or ever wanted to hear again.

A few days later, Marty and I were out in "Kandie's" dog kennel. She was a beautiful white pit-bull. This little girl was extremely muscular and highly energetic. Being that she had such a strong prey drive, we had to keep her separated from all the other dogs. This day, Marty and I had gone out to spend some time with her and throw the Tennis ball.

Marty had built the dog kennels himself, so there would be plenty of room for them to get exercise on the days we couldn't walk them. Kandie's kennel was an easy sixteen by thirty. I noticed there were big chunks of asphalt on the ground inside her kennel yet it was a good sixty yards from the road. It looked as if it had been pulled up from the edge of our driveway and thrown at her. Now, who would be throwing rocks at one of my dogs? I assumed it had to be the neighborhood kids, and I was ready to start calling parents when Marty told me there was no way a kid could have thrown anything that far. Well, maybe the asphalt had been here all along, and she had just dug it up? I was sure that was not the case. However, I had no proof. So that's what I went with. I still did not like the idea of someone possibly harassing my dog. Especially one that already had dominance issues.

That night, Marty and I were woken up once again to a blood-curdling scream. This scream came from the direction of the back yard. Our windows were all closed, and the central air was running when this horrible scream reverberated through our bedroom, shaking us both out of bed!

We hit the floor running for the back door. (The direction, the scream had come from,) I had no clue what was going on. However, that was the most horrible scream I had ever heard in my life! Just as Marty and I got to the back door, it opened, and Cari steps inside. We were both shocked to see her there. Had she been outside with this horrible scream? I knew there was no way she had made this noise. There was just no way a human could make noise this loud. I had felt this scream, as much as I heard it. Cari is white as a sheet and visibly trembling.

"Are you OK?" I asked.

She nods her head, yes. All I could do was wrap my arms around her. After she had calmed down a bit, we all went into the kitchen and sat down at the table.
There was still too much adrenaline running through our veins to even consider sleeping just yet. Cari begins to tell us what happened. As she talks, you can hear the terror in her voice.

Her little dog crying outside had woken her up. She said it was a strange cry. Therefore, she was very concerned about her. She had tried a few times to wake Chris. But, he continued to sleep soundly.

She got out of bed to check on her dog. There was some light coming from my parent's streetlight in the yard. It does not quite reach our backyard, making that area of the yard dim. With her back to the woods, she had just reached over the two-foot fence to pick up her dog, when that God-awful scream erupted just behind her.! She turned quickly to come face to face with... nothing. There was nothing there! Where she was standing was about ten feet from the woods. And that scream vibrated things in our bedroom! We all speculated on what could have made such a noise. Also, why did it scream just as she reaches her dog? Could she have interrupted an animal about to make a meal out of her dog?

We did not have any answers. However, one thing was for sure. We heard the scream. It was the most horrible sound I have ever heard.

Two days later, it was mid-morning. I had just gotten up and made myself a cup of coffee, while Marty slept in. A very sleepy Chris came into the kitchen, followed close behind by an even sleepier Cari. They both proceeded to the coffee pot. I am wondering why in the world they looked so sleepy. Maybe one of the babies had a rough night and kept them awake. I gave them time to be seated at the table. Then I asked. "So," what kept you two up last night?"Chris looks at me over the rim of his cup, with bloodshot eyes.

Cari responds, "Oh, nothing, but the sound of the back porch being ripped off our house."

I am shocked. What in the world is she talking about? Chris said," every time we would fall asleep, it would sound like something big would get a hold of the back porch and just pull it back and forth. It was loud, too. I'm surprised it didn't wake you guys up."
I am even more shocked now. "Did you look outside?" I asked.

Chris lets out a big yawn.
" I did, but it was too dark to see anything."

I was thinking that maybe an animal had gotten on the back porch and was making a noise that they weren't used to hearing. What else could it have been?

Later that day, I am doing my usual housework. I go to sweep off the back porch. Now, where in the world is my rug? I had bought a new rug for the backdoor just days before. Now it was gone. How could it just disappear? Our front and back yard were completely fenced in. A gate separated the front yard from the back yard. The fence stopped just at the side of my porch. Meaning, if you were very tall, you could stand in the yard and reach the porch railing without being inside the fence. However, you would have to be at least six feet tall to reach up to the railing. It was very high off the ground. There was no way anyone could reach over that railing. You would have to be at least nine feet tall. Pondering this, I knew we had not let any dogs into the back fence, as they usually carry off my rug.

Now, this is puzzling. I finally stop the dogs from stealing my rugs. How could it be gone again? I asked Marty and the kids if they have seen it. They are just as confused as I am. Could an Opossum or Raccoon climb my porch? Probably. But how would they drag off a rug?

I went back to my chores, the rug is forgotten until late that afternoon. Marty and I had decided to go to town and pick up some dinner. We get to the end of our driveway, and just before, we pull out onto the road. I see my rug! It is lying at the top of our yard, outside the fence. How in the hell did this happen?

'Marty, Look!" I said, pointing to the rug. Marty gets out of the car and walks over to it. He picks it up and looks at it. It is completely covered in mud and now unusable. He hangs it over the fence, to be thrown away when we get back.

We talk about this all the way to town. Neither of us can come up with a good explanation.

About an hour later, we return home. Marty stops as we pull into the driveway. I am going to walk over and check the mailbox while he gets the ruined rug.

I retrieve the mail and get back into the car. Marty slides back into his seat. We slowly start down the driveway. "I hope you threw that nasty rug on the floor," I said as I thumbed through the mail.

"Nope," he replies. I look up at him. "It's gone." He says.

"Gone?" "What do you mean, Gone?" I ask

"As in," "It's no longer there." He says.

"OK," "so maybe one of the kids picked it up," I think aloud. I knew this was not true. Why would they walk all the way up the driveway to get a rug they did not even know was there? But where else would a large muddy rug go?

I go into the house, intending to ask the kids. However, the phone is ringing, the dogs are barking. The rug is completely forgotten. It is never seen again.

Marty and I were watching TV one night when my mother called. She said she had just been outside walking her dog when she saw something strange. My mom and dad have a small Datsun mix. She is kept in the house all the time, so when they take her out, she is usually ready to spend some time outside. They have to leash her for these walks, or she will surely head for the woods!

This night, her dog wanted no part of going outside. Mom said she had to carry her out of the house. Once outside, all she wanted to do was get back inside. Now Marty and I raise Pit Bulls. At this time, I had about six adults in my yard. My mom said none of these dogs were barking. Which itself is highly unusual. If anything approaches either of these yards. These dogs let us know loud and clear.

Just as my mom was starting to go back inside, she saw movement off to her right, which is the direction of our back yards. She strained to see what was out there past the light. She could make out a dark shape just outside the tree line. She said she did not know what it was, but it was very big. She had called to make us promise not to be outside until morning.

She said she did not know what this thing was. All she did know was that it was huge. Once again, I am wondering if we have a bear in the area. It is highly unlikely, but not impossible. She said she did not think this was a bear. It seemed a lot bigger to her. I asked her what she thought it was. She said she had no idea. She was not about to stay out there to get a better look. I can't say that I blame her.

A couple of years ago, Marty and I, along with Chris and Cari, joined a local paranormal team after we had some activity in our home. Many times, we would have team meetings at our house, where we would grill out and feed the members during our meetings. It made things more relaxed and informal to grill some food and sit around the yard. So we had a meeting here on Saturday. There had been plenty of food for everyone, and as usual, we had leftovers.

I was cleaning up after the meeting and had decided to take some of this food next door to my parents. I had my arms full, so Cari walked me out to open the gate for me. Just as I stepped outside the gate, I heard this very low growl.

It was off to my right, seeming to come from the metal carport, which was about ten yards from me. I could not see anything in the dark, so I kept walking.

Cari called out, "Did you just hear that?"

I did not answer her, as I did not want to stop and acknowledge it.

Cari caught up to me about halfway across the yard. She said again, "Did you just hear that, growl?" I told her I had, and I did not like the sound of it. It was nice to have her company for the rest of the walk. We made it to my mom's house and delivered the food. The two of us started back across the yard without speaking. Cari and I both were feeling uneasy. We made it past the carport. Nothing. Maybe whatever had been there was now gone. We were about ten feet from the gate to our yard when we heard the growl again. However, this time, it was different. It was a growl, yet it was guttural too. Almost as if a handicapped person was trying to form words and talk. This sound had come from directly behind us! My blood went cold. My heart jumped in my chest!

The hairs on the back of my neck stood up. Cari and I both scrambled to get inside the gate as quickly as we could. Then we made a beeline for the front door, never looking back. I knew in my heart if I looked back, I would see whatever had made that noise. I did not want to see it. Now I had my answer. This thing was not a bear. Could it have been a stray dog? Maybe it was an injured Coyote. I was trying to rationalize what we had just heard. I knew it was not any of the animals that lived in this region. What could have made such a horrible noise? And why had I felt such sheer terror at hearing it?

With all the strange things going on around here, you would think I had put the two together by now. But the thought of a bigfoot honestly never crossed my mind. As far as I was concerned, the closest I would ever be in one is on TV. They were mostly in the extreme North West, Right?

I am usually the first one up every morning. Therefore, I am the one that lets the dogs out into the fence. (Having the fence is pretty convenient, I can just open my front door and let my dogs out, knowing they are safe in the front yard.)

I had just gotten up, so I sleepily head for the front door. I unlock and open it, the dogs go out, and I close the door. I have done this for so many years. That I think my body just manually knows to do this, with no thinking involved. After they go out, I make my way to the bathroom, and then back to the kitchen to make coffee. This morning, about the time the coffee gets finished. One of our small dogs is scratching at the front door. Just as I am letting this one in, I see a movement from the corner of my eye. My other dogs are on the outside of the fence! How in the world did they get out there! I step out onto the front porch to call for them, and I see the gate, It Is standing wide open. How could that have happened? We never leave that gate open. The dogs would get out and head straight for the woods. We have had this happen, and it took days to find them. There is no way anyone in this family would leave that gate open. So why is it open now? It was closed when we had to let them out late last night. I walk out to the fence to call my dogs back in and flip the latch on the gate. Could we have had an intruder during the night? This thought leads me to think that I had better go check the lock on the back door to see if someone had tried to get in.

As I walk through the house, out my kitchen window, I can see my back gate standing wide open. What happened last night?

I go outside to close this gate too. I then go to examine the back door for pry marks. Nothing. Why would someone just open both of my gates? Was it kids purposely letting my dogs out? I was pretty sure there were no kids close by. Again, there was just no explanation for this.

Later, the same day, my mom had called, and she and I were just chatting about random things. I mentioned my gates being open. She told me that her Kennel door had been open this morning too. (My father owns a Pitbull, which he keeps in this kennel.) Their dogs' kennel door was open, but luckily, he has stayed inside his fence. What was even stranger, his gate had a bottom and a top latch. Both were open.

For the past few mornings, as she would go to feed him, she would have to look for his food bowl. It wasn't where it was supposed to be. Each morning, she would find his bowl outside the kennel five or six feet away.

Now I am wondering why kids would open all the gates around here. And how in the world was a kid getting the bowl out of the kennel? I knew there was just no way; this dog would allow a stranger to enter his kennel. He would be barking his head off and possibly land a serious bite to an unknown person. With that thought, I knew there were a few of my dogs that would bite if approached by a stranger in the middle of the night. So how were kids quick enough to get the gates open and avoid being bitten?

Our gates would still be opened randomly. We never caught anything on the camera. Either the camera would be shifted, or it would turn off. (We found that strange. There were just no answers as to why it didn't get any good pictures.) Then my mom discovered something that none of us could explain.

Not long after this incident with the gates. My mother had gone out one morning to feed the dog (Cody). His collar had been removed and hung on the fence! Now, these are heavy-duty nylon collars. After closer inspection, the metal buckle that fastens the collar was bent in half. Marty said that it could not be done without a pair of pliers.

He checked Cody's neck anyway. If he had removed the collar himself, his neck would be injured. He did not have a spot on him. Even if he did remove his own collar, how did he hang it up?

By now, I was really starting to wonder about things going on around our house. Could it be paranormal? I would make a point to talk to Marty in private. We had some paranormal issues in the past. But they were always inside the house. Who was messing with us, and why? We had lived here for many years with our dogs and had never had any problems.

Our family was sitting around the table, having coffee that evening. The four of us, Marty, Chris, Cari, and I start discussing all the strange things that had gone on. We realized that the Crickets and bullfrogs no longer sang at night. The nights were very still now. In fact, it was so quiet it was almost eerie.
Another thing was the roadkill; we have not had any roadkill on our road for many years. This is strange since we live so rurally.

Last summer, we had noticed an abundance of rabbits in our yard at night.

There were so many that we actually joked about every rabbit in the woods coming to our yard. If you pulled into the driveway at night, the car lights would light up hundreds of rabbit eyes. I mean there had to be fifty or more at any given time. If we walked outside the front fence at night, there would be rabbits running everywhere! We all found this strange but figured they must have just been multiplying as rabbits do.

Marty had been sitting out back one evening, enjoying the breeze.

"Hey, Babe!" "Do you have a minute?" He called from the back door.

"Sure," I said, getting up from my computer.

"You are not going to believe this." He said,
As we both stepped out onto the back deck.

He pointed across the yard to the tree line. Oh my god! My eyes could not believe what they were seeing.

The owls had come back. There had to be twenty
Owls perched in the trees just at the edge of our back
yard. They were so beautiful.

"Why are they here?" I whispered. (Whispering just
felt right at the moment.)

"I don't know," Marty responded. "I don't understand
this at all. I don't know why they are behaving this
way."

For the following weeks, they would show up about
five in the evening and then leave at sunrise. Some of
our friends came over just to see this weird act of
nature.

I finally called the DNR again to see if there was
anything we could do to make them leave. Once
again, we pretty much had to deal with it. Luckily,
after a couple of weeks, they just stopped coming. I
was very grateful for this. Those are big predator
birds, and I feared for my grandson's safety.
Especially with them already acting strangely.

With all the things happening around here, you would
think I had derived a conclusion by now. However,
the thought of a bigfoot honestly never crossed my
mind. As far as I was concerned, the closest I would
ever be to one is on TV.

They were mostly in the extreme North West, Right?
And there was no hard proof that the creatures
actually exist. So in reality, why would I consider a
Bigfoot? For me, that would have just been insane.

One Morning Marty and Chris were just about ready
to leave for work. They got to the end of the driveway
and stopped. It looked as if a dog had been hit in the
road, at the edge of our yard.

Marty and Chris got out of the truck to go have a
better look. They decided they couldn't just leave the
animal lying there. It would be in the mid-nineties by
noon. This thing would surely smell up the yard. So
they came back to the house to get a rope and
shovel. On seeing them come back, I walked outside
to see what was going on. I guessed one of them
must have forgotten something. They both hop out of
the truck and start toward our utility building.

"So," "what did you forget?" I asked.

"Nothing," Chris said. "There has been a Coyote hit
on the road. We're going to bury it so it won't smell."

"Really?" I asked. I had never seen a Coyote up close. I walked across the yard with them. As we neared the animal, I could tell it was huge. However, I did not know until I was standing over her, just how big she was. This was an older female. She had the calluses on her leg joints that older dogs get. Marty tied her back legs with the rope so they could drag her off. She was much too large to pick up. Marty started to pull; she did not budge at all. Chris then grabbed the rope to help pull. She barely moved with both of them pulling! This was one large Coyote. And I couldn't figure out how she was hit. She was laid up in our yard. A good fifty feet from the road. There was no blood at all. None on the road and none of the grass where she had been laying. I was thinking, with her being so old, maybe she just died of old age. But wouldn't they go off privately somewhere to die? Could she have had a heart attack? Do dogs in general, even have heart attacks? While I am pondering these questions, Marty and Chris have decided to get the four-wheeler to pull her. They tie the rope to the four-wheeler and begin to drag her. This girl looked to be a good six feet long. That is with her back and front legs extended. I was shocked! I never knew they could grow that big. I was still wondering how she died.

I went back to the house while Marty and Chris dug her hole. I knew with an animal that size, the digging would take awhile.

Later the guys finished their task and headed off to work. The Coyote was forgotten until things started adding up for me. This was not long after. However, I still wonder. Would a Bigfoot break a Coyote's neck? And why, if it didn't intend to eat her?

As I mentioned earlier, the whole family are members of a paranormal team. (I know that some people seem to think the Paranormal and Bigfoot are tied together. I cannot say yes or no to that theory. All I can do is tell you about our own experiences.) Because of the activity in our home, we had called upon Dennis and Brandon for help.

Discussing the current happenings with them, we decided to put together a Cryptid group. As luck would have it, some of our current members were also interested in Cryptids.

We thought that since we had a large area of woods, it would be a great place to do some basic training with our new members.

After some debating on the name.

The Carolina Cryptid Crew was born on June first, twenty thirteen. http://Carolinacryptidcrew.com

One Saturday afternoon, I was working on my computer, and Marty had decided to take a walk through the woods to pick out the direction he wanted to lead the team in and to make sure it would be easy for people to navigate. I guess he was gone for about an hour; he came in and sat down next to me. When I looked up at him, I could tell something was up.

He says, "You are not going to believe what I found!" I can tell by his voice; it is something amazing. Then he asks me where the video camera is.

"It's in our Investigation bag," I tell him.

Without explaining why he was so excited, and just what it was that he had found. He takes the camera and leaves again.

He is gone for about an hour and a half. When he gets back, he loads the thumb drive onto his computer. Cari and I are both looking over his shoulder. So far, I am watching a video of him walking through the woods.

Then very slowly, he pans the camera for a very slow and amazing effect. My eyes are playing tricks on me. It cannot be! On the screen, Right in front of my face, is a Bigfoot tree structure! I have seen this many times on the Bigfoot videos. But in our woods? I am shocked. I am amazed. I am thrilled. I am confused, and even a bit frightened, all in one. It was that feeling of, I must be dreaming.

"Marty, did you do this?" I asked. Knowing before I asked that he didn't do it. Something like this would have taken him a few hours to accomplish.

"No way!" He responds. "I am just as amazed as you guys are." "I knew you would never believe me. That's why I came back for the camera."

While watching this video, I see two more tree
structures. (Could kids have done this? I knew we did
not have any kids that lived near us. However, my
brain was frantically searching for a logical
explanation.) There were also some arched trees, and
they were intricately woven together at the top. The
top of these trees was about ten to eleven feet high!
(I knew in my heart, there was just no way Marty or
kids could have done this.)

I wanted to see these things for myself. However, it
had started to rain. I was still in shock at what I had
just seen. Marty said, to start with, he could not
believe what he was looking at. Then when he came
across two more, he knew he had to get the camera.
But in these woods? How? Why? These things do not
live in South Carolina. Do they?

That night I emailed Dennis and Brandon. I told them
what Marty had found and included the video. It was
only a few moments wait until they both responded.
They both wanted to see this for themselves.
Therefore, we planned for them to come over one
evening a few days away. In the meantime, we were
to scout around for any other signs.

Marty, Cari, and I had made a couple of trips out into the woods to look around. Just to see if we came up with anything else. We came across a small area that was bare of trees. The ground was mostly red clay here, so we thought it would be a good place to look for footprints. I remember the three of us walking around this area with our heads down, being very careful where we stepped.

My eyes went to something that looked like a heel print, oh my. Further up, it got wider, yes, that's where the toes would be. I am standing here looking at a very large, bare footprint. All sorts of emotions flooded through me in a split second. I stepped back and looked again. It was unmistakable. It validated the tree structures. It was here! Or it had walked through here! Was it watching us now? I felt the small hairs on the back of my neck stand up. I slowly looked up and peered into the darkened woods. It could very well be standing in the shadows where the sun doesn't penetrate.

"Hey guys, come here!" I knew they could hear the emotions in my voice. They were both by my side in seconds, looking down to see what It was.

"OH MY GOD!" Cari exclaimed.

"Get the ruler," Marty said.

I handed him the ruler. He knelt down to measure the abnormally large print. (Sixteen inches long five across). The length could have passed for a man, but not the width.

It was a very strange feeling to be standing there looking down at this big footprint, knowing that the huge animal that made this had walked through here. Our home was not all that far away. I wasn't sure how I felt about this. I just couldn't fully accept what I was seeing. It was right there in my face, and I still couldn't accept that we may have a Bigfoot nearby. My mind was not willing to accept what my eyes had just seen. The three of us continued to look for more prints. We found another one the same size, then a smaller one. I still could not believe it. We took photos and videos of these footprints. But they just weren't deep enough to cast. I would have loved to be able to make a cast of what we had just witnessed. But I guess it was not meant to be.

When I got back in the house, the first thing I did was email Brandon and Dennis. I sent them the photos. The six of us planned to get together the following evening. And check the woods out more thoroughly.

When Brandon and Dennis arrived, We set up our grill at the edge of the woods and roasted some hot dogs. It has been said that the smell of a grill can bring Bigfoot in closer. As we ate our hot dogs, we chatted about Bigfoot and the strange things we had found in the woods.

My parents were babysitting my grandson that evening. They left around seven-thirty to take him to McDonald's for dinner.

I have chosen to keep my grandson's name private in this book. I will refer to him as Mack.

I had no idea that this particular event would have such bearings on the evening's evidence. But it does.

We finish our hot dogs, and the team heads out to the woods. Cari and I were setting up a live feed for the night. We were going to be streaming our first BigFoot hunt. So we had hung back to work on the computers.

It had just started getting dark. There was still a bit of light left in the yard. However, inside the tree line, night had already fallen.

I am sitting at the table with my back towards the woods. And Cary is facing me. As we were working, something hit the storage building just to my left. It sounded like an acorn had fallen and rolled down the roof. But this was in June. It couldn't have been an acorn. And I didn't think a stick would make that rolling noise. Oh well, I stopped wondering and went back to work. About sixty seconds later, something hit the storage building on my right.

 There were no trees at all around this building. Therefore, I knew the acorn or stick theory didn't hold here.

Cari asked, "Did you just hear that?"

"Yep," I said. "I'm starting to wonder what's making these noises."

We joked about having things thrown at us. As we laughed about this, something hit the charcoal bag, which was sitting near my leg. I was up and out of my chair! That had landed way too close to me! I was positive, then, we had just had a rock thrown at us! I could see it lying there on the ground by the bag. I wondered if someone was playing a joke on us. Without even speaking, as we knew what the other was thinking. Cari and I grabbed a walkie-talkie, a camera, and a digital recorder. We headed toward the dark woods. A few feet in, we heard a very distinguishable, "WHOOP!" I do not know how to explain the sound. However, you just knew it was not a bird. We had never heard that sound before.

Cari keyed the walkie-talkie and asked if any of our teams had heard a whoop. The team that was on the swamp responded that they had heard it too.

Just as the walkie-talkie went silent, we hear our first wood knock. I tell you, hearing it, so audible was almost surreal. I cannot describe all the emotions that ran through me hearing that single knock. Cari keyed the mike to tell the teams what we had just experienced. I slowly reached out and lowered her arm.

"They probably won't believe us," I said

We had just heard what many people would love to hear. However, I knew, no one would ever believe us. I knew in my heart. I had just experienced a Bigfoot knock.
I mean, what were the chances of our first time out, getting rocks thrown, hearing a whoop and a wood knock? It took me quite a bit of thinking to believe it myself. It was just too perfect. Could someone be messing around in the woods? But no one knew that we were doing this. Also, we had quite a few people out there in the woods. Therefore, that pretty much ruled out a prankster.

I realized then that I had heard this sound many times before. It was mostly in the summer months when I was laying out in the sun. I had often wondered what someone was working on to just give the occasional single knock. I had been hearing this sound for years and never realized what it was.

Cari and I then headed back to the table to get our video setup. A couple of hours later, the guys came back, all excited and hyped up, they too had heard the wood knocks and whoops coming from different locations. To our surprise, they had also found some footprints! Just as we were discussing the possibilities of casting them, Lightning flashed overhead. Storms were moving in.

Therefore, the best we could do at his time is to try to shelter the prints from the rain and hope for the best. That is exactly what we did. Marty and Chris would check the next day after the rains stopped to see what, if anything, we could save.

I woke up the next morning to the sound of rain. The first thing I thought of was those prints. Then my heart skipped a beat as my mind went to the events of the past evening, the rocks, the whoop, the knock.... After everyone had left, Cari and I told Marty and Chris what had happened and what we had heard. I am sure they believed us. However, I would not have blamed them for being skeptical. That was an awful lot to happen in one night. Some people spend years trying to experience this.

I remember all of us sitting at the kitchen table that day, discussing the possibilities of a Bigfoot in our woods. We talked about the past signs that we had not paid attention to;

The screams in the middle of the night.

The missing rug.

The disappearing turkeys.

The dead coyote.

The Owls.

The Rabbits.

The silence of the frogs and crickets.

The missing roadkill.

The tree structures.

The back porch being shaken.

The gates being opened.

The large shadows at night.

The Squirrels being gone.

The neighbors were missing dogs.

All the unexplained things were starting to add up now. And now, even though it sounded crazy, we were almost positive that it was there. The only thing missing at this point was seeing one.

The rains finally stopped at about noon that day. Marty and Chris went out to check on the prints, and see if anything could be saved, there was actually very little left, we got some photos, but no actual cast, we were so disappointed.

Later that day, Cari and I went next door to get Mack, as he had stayed the night with my parents. We were telling them about the events of the evening. As it turned out, they had quite a story to tell us.

The night before When they had left to take our grandson to McDonald's They had stopped at the stop sign at the end of our road. Just to their right, it appeared as if some large animal had gotten hit on the road. They sat there for a few minutes waiting for traffic and trying to make out what this animal was. They said there was an old pickup truck pulled off to the shoulder along with a Deputy Sheriff car. The men were in the middle of the road looking at the animal. The sheriff deputy noticed them sitting at the stop sign, so he walks over to his car, gets in, and pulls it in-between them and the animal.

Since they can no longer see the animal, my parents drive off in the opposite direction, not thinking much more about it. They have both stated that it was too big to be a horse, a cow or a bear. They also described it as being very dark.

After talking it over with our team, we decide to call the Sheriff's Dept and the DNR to see if there was a report. Cari called our local sheriffs department and was told that she would need to call the DNR. She hangs up and calls the DNR.

She gave them the name of the highway and asked them if a large animal had been hit on that specific date. The woman on the phone stated that she would have to speak with her supervisor before she could give out that information. She took Cari's name and phone number. We waited a few days for this return phone call.

 Finally, when the call came in, It was the supervisor himself. Instead of giving us any information, he just drilled Cari.
Who was she?
Why did she want to know?

What was her address?

Who told her to call them? So forth and so on. He ended a million questions with, I am sorry, but we have no report on this. I smell something fishy here. After this phone call, I was more than sure that they knew something. I asked a friend "on the inside" to do some digging for me. I was told that there had been a report made on that specific date. However, it had since been deleted. What is up with this? Why would they delete a report on an animal getting hit on the road? Just what was it that they did not want us to know about? We knew now that we would never get that information.

So all we could do was forget about it. Marty, Cari and I had made a couple of trips out into the woods to look around. Just to see if we came up with anything else. We found some more large footprints. And again, I had a hard time accepting what was right in front of my face. And I felt the flood of all these different emotions. Just how are you supposed to feel when you find evidence that these creatures are very close to your home? There is no handbook for this.

We called Dennis and Brandon to tell them about the footprints. After discussing it, we decide to try to cast these. They came over, and we made another trip out to the woods. We poured the cast and waited. I am sure we were all praying that they would come out to be perfect prints. Well, they didn't turn out as well as we would have liked. Nevertheless, we hoped they would be better once they were cleaned up. Dennis was our man for this job. We wrapped each one in a large trash bag, and then placed them in a cardboard box. He would take them home with him and work on them over the next few days.

After the guys had left, I went in to work on my computer. That is when I noticed my email had was hacked. This was the email I used to contact Dennis and Brandon. We had talked a lot about BigFoot through emails. I told my daughter in law, so she decided to check hers as well. As we suspected, hers had been hacked too. Coincidence? Maybe.

Later that night is when things really got strange.

Dennis said he had gone to bed around ten that night. And his little dog woke him up over in the wee hours of the morning, barking like mad. This was very unusual for this dog. He was barking as if he had seen someone. Dennis got up to check it out.

That is when he heard footsteps running away. Also, he saw that his back gate was open. Earlier in the evening, he had checked that gate to make sure it was closed. Living in town, he did not want to take a chance on his dog getting out. You also had to go through the garage to get to this gate. Thinking about that is what made him remember that the Bigfoot casts were still in his truck. He immediately went to retrieve them and bring them inside for the night.

Two days later, Marty and I were coming home from town. It had been raining hard all day. We turned onto our road, started down the hill to the bridge, and stopped. Right in front of us, blocking the bridge was a fire truck along with a few other trucks. Men were standing on the bridge, in the pouring rain talking.

This was strange, as this bridge is about five hundred yards from our house. Therefore, I grab my camera and start snapping off a few shots. (I always have my camera with me.) The men turn to look at us, so we start to back slowly up. I was snapping pictures the whole time. We left, drove around the block, and came onto our road from the other direction. We slowly drove past our home to the top of the hill, we could see down to the bridge from here. The men were still standing in the middle of the bridge talking. And the rain was coming down in buckets!

This made absolutely no sense to me at all. I snapped a few more pictures from this direction. Then we went home. I immediately email Dennis and Brandon, sending them a few of the pictures. Dennis advised us to be cautious.

Cari called the Highway Department the following morning. She told them she had noticed the men on the bridge, and wondered if she should be concerned with the structure of the bridge. They told her the bridge was perfectly safe. So now, we know they were not planning to work on the bridge.

Marty, Cari, and I would get out to the woods every
few weeks to see if we could spot anything. Almost
every time we would head out to comb the woods,
there would be a plane or drone flying low, just above
the tree line. It appeared as if they too were looking
for something.

As I mentioned before, we were learning a lot from
watching YouTube videos. However, some things may
not be so good for a newcomer. (Having warnings on
these videos would be a good idea. Sort of like a
"Swim at your own risk," sort of deal.)
Before, I go any further; Let me say, there are some
very knowledgeable people in the Bigfoot community.
There are some amazing videos out there. Like
anything else, you cannot believe everything you hear
or see. When using YouTube for learning about
Bigfoot / Sasquatch, throw a large amount of
common sense in with it.

We had watched a few videos where people had made
gifting stumps. Therefore, we thought this might be a
good way to get some interaction going.

Now I look back and wonder, why in the world did I ever think it would be good to interact with something that is along the same lines as an enormous wild animal with superhuman strength? What was I going to do if this thing decided he liked the treats and followed me home? As you can now see, this was not well thought through. And the worst part is, my family went along with me! Not one of us thought, maybe this is not a good idea. (Looks like common sense may have eluded all of us.)

We gathered up some apples, granola bars, and a jar of peanut butter. We took our food supplies out to a tall stump in a secluded section of the woods. Here there was dense vegetation, and it took quite a bit to get to it. We figured this would be a good place to set up our gifting stump. Any animal showing up would have a hard time being spotted, and the stump was about waist high, so maybe that would deter some smaller critters.

Marty unscrewed the lid of the peanut butter jar, then he replaced it with only one turn if anything got into it, it would have to be able to screw the cap off. I opened one Granola package and left the other sealed. Of course, we set up the trail cam to face the stump. I knew there was a little to none chance that we would actually catch anything. But I guess it never hurts to try. We gave it a few weeks, and Marty went to check the stump and retrieve the camera.

The food we had left was gone; in its place were three blackbird feathers. Now I know that this could have happened naturally. However, the fact that they were lying in a row, the same distance apart, was strange. The peanut butter jar was completely gone, with the lid lying at the base of the stump. The lid had not been chewed or broken. Marty left more food and got the trail cam. We were all so anxious to see what the cam had captured. We watched Marty's computer excitedly; We had some pictures of deer. And A Raccoon helped himself to some food. An Opossum waddled by. Then a Little red fox came to check out the food. That was all we had captured this time, just normal forest animals.

Again, we left the food for a few weeks before checking it. This time Cari and I tagged along with Marty. I thought I saw something out of place as we neared the stump.

The closer we got, the more I was sure of it. We slowly picked our way through the dense undergrowth. Just a couple of feet past our stump was a new tree structure! I pointed it out to Marty and Cari.

"Look at these guys." "Looks like we have had some activity," I said.

Marty went ahead of us to get a better look.
"Look at how the leaves are packed down," he said.

Sure enough, the ground looked as if something had been walking all around the tree structure. All the leaves were packed down about three feet out in all directions. Cari and I got busy snapping photos while Marty put out some fresh food.

https://www.youtube.com/watch?v=DF23v-ygTvQ

We were still snapping photos when Marty noticed something about ten feet from the stump. Well, look at this, he said as he was walking toward an object Cari and I couldn't see. He bent to pick up something. Walking back toward us, I saw the empty Peanut butter jar in his hand. It had not been chewed on at all, but it was empty. We speculated how an animal could get all the peanut butter from the bottom of the jar. None of us had any good explanations. I had walked a few feet away from the stump still snapping some photos, as I panned my camera, I could not believe what I saw. Why hadn't I seen this earlier? It was a very large X made with two trees that had been pulled out of the ground and placed there in a small clearing.

"Hey, guys, Look," I said. Pointing in the direction of the X.

"Now that's new," Marty said.

We all knew it, and the structure had been done in the last few weeks, but we had no clue as to what this meant.

We tried again with the peanut butter jar. Again, the jar was cleaned out and left laying a few feet from the stump. Our webcam was somehow shifted, so it was recording a few feet to the left of the stump. Nothing at all was captured.

Marty, Cari and I were still doing random sweeps of the woods, trying to collect as much evidence as possible.

Every time we go out in the woods now, we are equipped with cameras and digital recorders. As we are walking, I keep turning behind us and snapping photos. (Thank you, Scott Carpenter.) He was the first person I had ever seen do this. And it was like a light bulb went off. Most people don't think to do this. But you never know what might be following you.

I had just started to turn behind us and snap a few photos, when I saw this tree moving, about fifteen yards away. And this thing was moving back and forth pretty quickly. (It appeared as if something was in the underbrush at the base of the tree, whipping it back and forth. The tree itself would be roughly a circumference of eight inches.)

It was right in the middle of some very thick undergrowth that was over waist-high. It was too dense to see into it. Marty and Cari had just passed by here. I had gotten a few steps behind them by stopping to take photos. I call out to them, "Hey!" "We have some movement over here."My heart was pounding. Not knowing if this was going to be some wild animal that may be trying to protect its home. We had no weapons with us. I guess it hadn't occurred to us that we may need one.

They both turn and look in the direction I am looking. The tree is barely moving now. I quietly point toward the tree. Marty and Cari both nod their heads, signaling, they saw it. We all three start slowly walking in that direction. It was down a slight slope from the path we had been walking on. Therefore, we were now walking at an angle to get to it. As luck would have it, my camera chose to die just then. I start to walk backward back up this incline, keeping my eyes glued to the spot. I assumed if I walked back up this incline, I would be able to see a bit better than Marty or Cari could.

Marty went to the left of this undergrowth, Cari to the right. It was then that I saw something Cinnamon colored moving from the undergrowth going further into the woods. I could not make out what it was, as I only saw glimpses of fur through the vegetation. It appeared to be walking on four legs or crawling. My mind automatically thought bear. But we don't have many bears in our area, and if we do, it's a black bear. Then I think of a cow. No, a cow would be making much more noise whatever this was made no noise at all when it moved. I am trying to rationalize this into something my mind can explain. Being slightly above Marty and Cari, I could see further. I yell out that I saw something moving. I wanted them to be aware that there was some animal close to them so that they could be prepared. Cari, being on the right side, was directly in front of me. About twenty feet from what I was seeing. Marty is to the left, was further away, and blocked by the vegetation. He is asking me how far away it is. I can hear the urgency in his voice. I heard him asking me this repeatedly while he is trying to get a good shot with his camera. But I couldn't answer; I had just locked eyes with something that appeared halfway human!

About 20 yards from where I stood, There were trees, vines, and underbrush grown together to form a thick wall. There was a very slight opening here, and this is where it and I made eye contact. The side of the head came into view; first, my eyes only saw hair, and I did not know then that it was the side of this creature's head. I watched it turn to its right, I could see the face, the head, and the top of the right shoulder, as it turned to look at me, its shoulders moved with it. We locked eyes for what seemed like an eternity. I no longer heard any sound around me. I was looking into these dark eyes...A strong wave of sadness flooded through my entire body. Why was this creature so sad? The sadness I felt was overwhelming. No fear, no excitement, just a horrible sadness. I can hear Marty's urgent voice, but I can't answer him. I am fixated on this creature, the time has stood still. The eyes said, do not follow me. I knew that as if someone had just spoken it out loud. Do not follow me. Then it was gone. It moved forward and was gone. "Do not follow me." Did I hear this in my head, or read it on its face? I have no idea.

I am well aware of how stupid this may sound as you read it. But I am telling you exactly as our encounter happened.

It felt like I stood there forever, just looking at where that face had been. My mind was not accepting what had just happened. I knew in my heart what had just taken place, but my mind was not ready for this reality. This had just shaken my whole belief system. Now, for me, monsters were real. Monsters did exist.

It's gone, I said quietly. Marty heard the change in my voice and turned to look at me. Cari still stared quietly at the opening in the brush. Had she seen this too? When Cari turns to look at me,

I calmly say," What did you just see?"
She looks me dead in the eye and says,
"I just saw a Bigfoot."
I can tell by her expression that her mind has not yet accepted what her eyes have just seen.
She tells me it was Cinnamon colored with sad eyes. My heart skipped a beat. What she said next, let me know that she saw exactly what I did.
"Its face had a sadness to it." "A sadness I cannot explain." And its eyes said, "Don't follow me."

Marty is standing there with his camera in hand, looking at us both like we have just lost our minds.

I tell him what I just saw, and he turns to go in the direction this creature had been. I grab his arm, "No!" I said. "We can't follow her." (I have no idea if this was a male or a female that is just the feeling I got.) Now I had to explain to him the feeling I had gotten from her eyes. I guess if he had thought I was crazy earlier, I just confirmed that for him.

Without speaking, we all turned to start the walk back home. Each of us was in our own way, dissecting what had just transpired. I don't believe any of us spoke the whole way home. Maybe Marty did, he kept kicking himself for not being on the right side of the underbrush to get the photo.

At first, I was disappointed that we didn't get one too. But looking back now, I believe I would have torn it up. These things have lived here peacefully for many years. Who are we to disturb them and disrupt their lives? I also have no need to prove anything. I know they exist, and that is enough for me.

I honestly can't remember if I emailed Dennis and Brandon about our encounter. I don't think I did, as I remember this changing everything I had felt before.

I was no longer in a big rush to find more footprints and to find more evidence. It would show up in time. They were here. I had that confirmed for me. So now, the need to prove it exists was completely gone.

*Note. Please, do not let my encounter cause you to believe these creatures are harmless. I feel that, like any wild animal, they should be treated with caution and respect. When you are in the woods, you are in their territory. And you just may be an unwanted guest.

The next time Marty went out to check or gifting stump, about five weeks had passed. The guys had been working late in the evenings, and we had forgotten to check it. When Marty came back, he said it looked as if a tornado had gone through the woods. Of course, I asked him what he meant by this. He said the trees near the stump were totally destroyed. I got him to walk back up there with me so I could see what he was talking about. Sure enough, it looked as if something big was very pissed off. (But why? Why had this thing gone into such a rage?)

I guess the best way to explain it would be something very big threw a temper tantrum and pushed over trees for a good two acres. It was completely bare. And right in the middle of where the trees had been was a solitary X. What do these X's mean? I was so full of questions and knew; I may never find the answers.

(http://carolinacryptidcrew.blogspot.com/2013/12/new-evidence.html)

I sent out emails to all the current members of our paranormal team. Extending an invitation to those interested in joining the Carolina Cryptid Crew. I set us up a web page and a Facebook page. Cari got us a twitter account up and going. Then we were ready to open up membership to the public. We had quite a few people contact us. It wasn't long, and we were ready for our first official expedition. Of course, we knew some woods that were the perfect place for the team to get their feet wet. We had decided to make this a training investigation for them. Get them used to the woods. Show them things to look for, like tree structures and arches.

Show them the difference in a bent weather tree and a force bent tree. Get them used to navigating the wooded terrain. We planned a Saturday night expedition.

Having had good results with the last time, we grilled out. We assumed it would be a good idea to once again use the grill, and place it just outside the tree line. Knowing that these creatures inhabited this land from time to time, there was a good chance that someone would have an experience that night. For this training expedition, we had nine people and divided up into three groups. One of our teams had been standing in the woods quietly listening. They heard something coming through the tree branches above them, and then it hit the ground with a thud. They turned on their flashlights and saw a rock that had not been there earlier. Turning their lights back off, the second rock came through the branches and struck the ground. With this one, they decided it was time to move before this thing got any more aggravated with them. There were a couple of knocks heard, but other than that, the night remained still. I guess they weren't up to "playing" with us that particular night.

It did not take long for the media to find out about our team. I guess there just aren't that many Cryptid teams in our area. So for our next couple of meetings, we had camera crews and newscasters following us through the woods. I think we did four news segments.

You can use the links below to see the news reports, they are still listed online as of today 7/24/14

http://www.counton2.com/story/24148938/group-claims-bigfoot-evidence-found-in-oconee-co

http://www.wbtw.com/story/24149762/group-claims-bigfoot

http://www.free-times.com/cover/carolina-bigfoot-021914
http://www.wyff4.com/news/local-news/oconee-pickens-news/group-opens-upstate-search-for-bigfoot/23500200#!bk6yr1

http://www.bigfootbuzz.net/oconee-sc-team-claims-bigfoot-photos-and-prints-found/

Most of them did a great job. But I was never comfortable with this at all.

I tried to stay back and just watch as some of them showed up and tried to make a public mockery of our team. Of course, we did become subject to the usual ridicule. If you choose to believe in something others don't, you are automatically crazy. I think so far, we have been called crazy and mindless rednecks. Yes, It does hurt to hear people say such cruel things. But we knew once we started our team that we would be subject to such remarks.

One good thing about the media is, it got our team name out there. It was not long until someone contacted us to do a cancer benefit. We are always available to help people, so that is what we did. The day of the benefit was beautiful. February 28, 2014. It was unseasonably warm, with clear blue skies. We all had a great time doing this benefit. And we wrapped it up about five that afternoon. We were driving home and discussing how well things had gone. During the drive, we had stopped to let traffic pass so we could make a turn. Just as we turned, I looked off to my right.

"I see something walking!" I exclaimed.

I had seen something walking in a ravine. It was heading toward the woods and a nearby lake. I could only see from the waist up. The color was the exact same color as the trees it was approaching. White, grey, and black. It appeared to have no neck, and the head was more oval than round. (Could it have been a man wearing a hoodie?) The way it moved just somehow did not look right. The chest and forearm were massively thick. Unlike anything, I had ever seen before. The head had no up and down movement with the walk. It just stayed even as it moved along. This could not be what I thought it was! It was daylight!

Marty turned to look at what I was seeing. His view was the same as mine, only from the waist up. Also, he was not quick to admit what he saw.
So on the way home, we go over all the options.
Was it a man? No.
Was it a bear? No.
Could it have been a Bigfoot? Possibly.

Since then, Marty has driven back by this area. He came home telling me that the ravine we saw this creature walking in was very deep. He said, as much as he hated to admit it, this thing had to have been over nine feet tall I have wanted to go back and see how deep this ravine is. Then go on down and explore the woods and lake. The Direction this thing had been walking was toward some chicken houses and a lake beyond them. After going back and examining the area, Marty now admits, he saw a Bigfoot.

A few months later, Some team members had gathered in the woods. Which is now called our "research area" for an overnight expedition.

We knew there was a very good chance of someone having an experience, if not an encounter. We had a dinner of simple grilled hot dogs and talked about the evidence we had found so far. As the sun faded and twilight turned into night. We headed out to the woods.

Marty, Cari, Jean, Laverne, Michelle, and I headed about fifty yards into the woods.

Chris and Brandon had left a bit earlier than the rest of us, to go and find a good spot to post up. As we got about fifty yards in, Cari and I moved off to the left. While the others went on about twenty-five more yards and passed the tent that Jean and Laverne had sat up earlier that evening. (They would be camping out here tonight. Hoping to catch a glimpse of something.)

Cari and I walked a bit further to find a spot to stand where there were not so many broken sticks and leaf litter. That way, if either of us moved, we would not be causing so much noise. We turned out our flashlights and waited. I told Cari to go ahead and turn on our Walkie-Talkie, where we would have access to the other team members, should we get any action. It was then that we found out that our walkie-talkie had this nice problem of turning itself off once you keyed the mike. Great! So we were alone now. I really did not have a real good feeling about this. The other two teams had weapons. We had nothing. We had no way to reach our team. And no weapon to protect ourselves with. As luck would have it, it was then that we heard the footsteps in the leaves.

They were coming up from the direction of a cane thicket that was further down on the property. These footsteps sounded about thirty yards away. They were steadily coming closer. And my heart was about to pound out of my chest!

Cari whispers, "Something is out there."

And she is looking in the direction of the footsteps. I risked a call out to my team. "Hey! We have movement."

No one answered. I was looking in the direction they had gone in. I could make out just a faint glow of a flashlight between the trees. Probably too far away to hear me. The steps are still coming in our direction. Like it was purposely walking toward us at a steady pace. I admit, hearing those footsteps coming at us like it had a purpose, sort of freaked me out a bit. They were rapidly approaching. And I knew that whatever this was would be on top of us in less than a couple of minutes! The only thing I could think to do was to turn on my light and start to walk toward it. Hoping this would deter it from approaching us. (This works for most wild animals.) I could only pray that it would work now.

Just as we took two steps in that direction, all hell broke loose! Something was coming down through the branches of the tree we had just been standing under. And it was coming fast! I could hear it hitting the branches as it came down. I whirled around and shone my light up into the tree. I saw something falling, but it was moving too fast for my eyes to focus on it. Then something hit the ground with a horrible thud! I shined my light down to the base of the tree. There now, lay a very large rock, about the size of a cinder block, which could have easily killed one of us, had we been hit in the head! And this rock would have had to come from our right. There must be two of them. And it seemed they both knew exactly where we were standing! The footsteps had stopped. It did not take long for us to decide to leave the woods and regroup, catch our breath and get us a walkie-talkie that worked.

We were both shook up at what had just happened. Marty was leading one of the other teams, as they were not quite used to the woods. Right then, I desperately wanted the comfort of having him with me. We left the woods and went back to the tables we had set up for food. These tables were located About twenty to twenty-five feet from the tree line.

Our lights had the area pretty well lit up.

We both grabbed a soda from the cooler and sat down at the table for a minute. We were going over what had just happened. The fact that one of us could have been seriously injured had my nerves on edge. This was no longer a fun thing to do. I quickly learned just how dangerous this could be. We checked out the remaining walkie-talkies. The few remaining on the table didn't work. We would have to do this with no team contact. A while later, we headed back out to the woods. We had walked in about ten yards and stopped to listen. The woods were deathly silent. My gut instinct told me we were not alone, and I had the unnerving feeling of being toyed with. I knew I did not want to remain in those woods. I have no idea why this was such an overwhelming feeling. I have learned from my Paranormal training, if you feel this way, it is best to go ahead and leave the area. Just as I was about to say something, Cari voiced her concerns. She was feeling that same unnerving feeling that I had. Therefore, we started out of the woods once more. On our way out, we heard a very distinctive tree knock. We instantly stopped to listen. I am assuming one of our team answered back with a similar tree knock. As we heard the second one not long after.

Then it was a whole trio of knocks! (Later, when talking with the team, we learned that they had only done two. And both of those had gotten a response. They did not make the rest of the knocks.

Cari and I returned to the tables. As far as I was concerned, I was done for the night. That feeling of impending danger had been just too strong for me to ignore it. I have never felt such an intense feeling about this as I had that night. Maybe I was still unnerved by the events. I do not know. However, I knew I was not going back out there that evening.

As we sat quietly at the tables, we kept our eyes on the tree line. You could feel something just beyond the light. I kept straining my eyes to see if I could catch a glimpse of what was watching us, but I never did.

Then I heard a deep breath come from the woods. It was almost human. It sounded like a large man would take a deep breath and let it out quickly. This sound continued from different points of the tree line for the remainder of the evening.

Not long after this odd breathing had started, small rocks started hitting the top of the metal garage. We could hear them hit and roll off. There were no trees above us. We knew it was rocks. Being that they were small, we could not seem to find them in the grass around the table. After what seemed like hours of us listening to this strange breathing, it stopped. Just then, we saw a flashlight growing brighter as it came through the woods. A teammate was returning. Apparently, they frightened away our visitor. It was Marty returning. He said that they had heard footsteps all around them most of the evening. And it felt like they were being surrounded. But when they would turn on their flashlight. It would be just out of reach of the light. He was positive it had been playing with them. Where he had been sitting, he was facing toward us. Therefore, the area he was looking into being lighter than where he sat. He said he had seen something moving back and forth at the tree line. He watched this shadow making random movements at the tree line most of the night. He was too far away to hear any footsteps. And since they were experiencing activity, he didn't want to risk getting up to check it out. (He had just unknowingly confirmed what Cari and I had been feeling.)

He told us that the other girls had gone to their tent for the night. It was going on two in the morning. So Cari and I decided to call it a night too. We would hear about the rest of the experience in the morning.

The next morning, some of our team members reported that they had chased random footsteps most of the night.

They would go after the footstep sounds only to have them totally stop with nothing there. At one point, they were listening to approaching footsteps. They said they came right up to them and stopped. They quickly turned on their lights, expecting to be face to face with something. But there was nothing there! As they stood silently listening to the random steps. They saw something tall in the shadows. It was only a dark silhouette. However, they watched it moving from the base of one tree to another, then look around the tree as if peeking at them. It squatted down seeming to hide. Then it was just gone.

The girls said that they had heard footsteps walking around their tent for a while after they lay down.

Then from somewhere deep in the woods came a horrible scream. They said it sounded as if an animal were being killed. It screamed once or twice, and then the woods were deathly silent again. We went to look, and the ground had been packed down all the way around their tent. Something had definitely been walking there. We had the trail cam pointed in that direction all night. Maybe it had captured something!

The trail cam turned out to be very disappointing. Apparently, it had somehow loosened itself during the night and was recording while facing down. I think our expedition that night interfered with something hunting its dinner. Then after we all settled down for the night, it found its prey.

We recently had some friends come in from Virginia to stay a few days with us on the fourth of July. The morning they were due to arrive, Chris was out cleaning our pool as he worked; he heard about six separate tree knocks coming from our woods. He told us that he knew that he was being watched. I'm not sure what had them so active this morning. They are usually pretty quiet until the early evening. But this particular morning they seemed to be stirred up.

One of our friends, Jennifer, is very intrigued with Bigfoot, so the guys took her out into the woods to show her some tree structures. She was amazed at how many there were and how intricately some were woven. I believe they heard a knock or two while they explored the woods. Luckily, this time, I didn't have to go. I stayed back with the others and watched the kids play in the swimming pool. I was uneasy about being out there again. I needed to give it more time.

We cooked out that night, as we thought the grill would stir things up, and maybe we would get a few yells or tree knocks for Jen and Danielle. Unfortunately, everything stayed quiet except for the crickets and frogs. They were unusually loud this evening. I had a feeling nothing would happen; the woods were just too loud. It sounded like a typical Summer evening with the loud sound of frogs and crickets. We watched as lightning bugs spotted the yard Jen wasn't too interested in entering the woods after dark, I really don't blame her. The woods had started to make me feel nervous too. I know there is something lurking out there just past our line of sight. And I know that it watches us without us seeing it. That reason alone is enough to keep most people out of the woods.

As we all sat in the lower part of the yard that
evening. Marty was cooking some chicken on the grill.
Just before the sunset, I noticed that Jen kept looking
past me during the conversation.

She was facing the woods while I sat facing her,
putting my back toward the woods. I asked her if she
saw anything. She strained her eyes and said, I just
keep seeing shadow play, but there is nothing there. I
keep getting the feeling like something is out there
watching us. But I just can't see it. I smiled and told
her that we get that feeling a lot here. You know
something is there, but your eyes just can't catch it,
so you keep staring, expecting to see it at any
second. We enjoyed our dinner and sat in the yard
talking until well after dark. Our forest friends decided
to remain hidden from our guests.

The next day Marty, Chris, and Jen headed back out
to walk through the woods. This time, they were told
to leave. They said they had walked a long way into
the woods to look for new tree structures. They all
three said they kept hearing something walking
through the leaves, but they never could see what it
was.

At one point they had stopped to talk, this is when they heard the footsteps again coming from a ravine down below them, the footsteps stopped, then the sound of a large tree breaking, falling and hitting the ground! Marty said the breaking was extremely loud. They decided this was their cue to leave the woods. We tried some tree knocks and a few yells. We almost always get a response, but not this time. The woods remained quiet except for the frogs and crickets again. I couldn't understand why the frogs and crickets had started up when they had been silent all summer.

That evening, once again, we were going to enjoy the shaded back yard and Marty was putting dinner on the grill. Danielle had brought her son with her, so he and our grandson were having fun playing in the pool and running around the back yard. It was nice to hear the laughter and squeals of little boys playing here again. It had been many years since Chris was young.

As we sat talking, one again, I saw Jen look past me into the woods, I turned around to look for myself and couldn't believe what I had seen.

I slowly got up to walk toward this new tree structure. It was just at the edge of our yard. Not even in the woods. Had these things actually been in our back yard?

I was not sure how I felt about this. I had known for quite some time that they were watching us. But to know that they had entered the yard sort of gave me the creeps. I walked to it, and Jen followed me. Marty showed me this one earlier today, she said. Apparently, Marty had already spotted this one but didn't want to alarm me, so he hadn't told me it was here. I looked back at the kids playing less than ten yards from me. I didn't like this at all. This was encroaching on my family space. But what had I been doing to them? Had I not brought strangers into their space? Had I not spent countless hours in the woods looking for them? Wow, what an epiphany. We were soon joined by Cari, who had walked up to see what we were looking at. Naturally, when Cari realizes what it is, she whips out her phone and starts snapping photos. This one is close, she says. Meaning it is close to our house. I know, I replied, it is probably why we haven't been told about it.

We examine it a few more minutes, then walk back into the yard. We return to our chairs, and the conversation changes. My mind is still on just how close this is. And when was this done? Had we been sleeping at the time? Had we been in the front yard? One of us could have easily walked out back and come face to face with whatever created this.

Our friends were due to leave the next day. I was disappointed that they had not got to experience the sounds that we hear almost daily; the wood knocks, the rock clacks the whoops and yells.

We all spent some time that morning having coffee on the front porch and planning our next get-together. These girls were very dear to my heart, and we didn't get to spend near enough time together, time and distance kept us apart. They left about noon that day, we all did our round of hugs and promises to get together soon.

The four of us sat down at the table on the front porch as our guests drove down the driveway. The moment the car was out of sight, we all heard a very loud tree knock! It came from the backside of our house. Why did they wait for our company to leave? Had they been watching our guests. We were all just shocked that this had happened at this exact moment. I thought of emailing them later on and telling them what had just happened. But I never got around to doing that. What purpose would it have served anyway? It never happened while they were here.

Later, Marty and I sat out enjoying the summer evening. The night was very still; there was absolutely no breeze blowing at all. I had been hoping for a thunderstorm as we desperately needed the rain. As we both sat reading on our tablets, we heard an extremely loud tree break coming from in front of us. The trees in our front yard blocked the view of the trees across the road. As loud as this was, I thought it had come from our front yard. I got that sudden feeling of terror as my blood went cold. This was way too close to us!

I was waiting on the loud thump of the tree hitting the ground, but it never came. On later inspection, we discovered a tree across the road from us that had been broken from about twelve feet up. The top did not just fall from this tree, the top had been twisted out. This had happened about forty yards from where we sat on our front porch. They seem to be getting closer to our house. I find that very unnerving. Upon further examination, this location was covered with Blackberry bushes and the ground is completely tramped down under the tree that was broken. I can't say what happened here as I only heard the noise. But from what we saw, there was no reason for this tree to have broken on its own.

Chris and one of his friends decided they wanted to check the woods out one night to see if there was any activity. Marty, Cari, and I came along for the walk. We were all equipped with flashlights and nothing else. (Now, I do not recommend this at all!) It was late at night when we got out to the woods, I'm guessing about eleven. The five of us begin to walk the left part of the woods. The further we walked into the woods, the more anxious I became. I didn't know why I felt this way. I had an underlying feeling that something wasn't right.

Suddenly we heard leaves crunching to our left, something, was moving in the underbrush. The trees were very thick in this area, so there was no way our flashlights could penetrate the darkness. We all stopped walking and stood silent listening. The noise stopped too. As we stood there holding our breath, fear crept up in my throat. Marty sensed that I was uncomfortable as he stepped up and slid his arm around my waist. Normally this would cause my fear to subside just knowing that he was this close to me. But this time, it didn't seem to work. We once again began walking further into the woods. With each step, my anxiety increased. I am always telling our team members in both the cryptid and the paranormal, that if you ever feel uncomfortable, you should leave at once. That is your body's warning signal. Why wasn't I heading this advice now? I knew if I decided to leave the woods that Cari would walk back with me as that is one of our strictest rules; no one walks alone in the woods after dark. The sound of footsteps in the leaves stopped my train of thought. Something big was walking alongside us. Just as my brain connected these footsteps with ours, everyone stopped.

Marty whispered, "It's over there."

He motioned in the direction I had heard these big steps coming from. Again, the woods were completely silent. Every time we would stop, whatever was walking beside us would stop too. As we stood there listening, I felt that something was about to charge us from the unseen depths of the woods. That did it,

I said, "I'm going to head back to the house."

Just as I said this, Cari followed with, "me too!"

She and I clasped hands and started making our way out of the woods. We were not letting go of the other one's hand! As we reach the safety of our back yard, Cari said, "I am so glad you said something about coming back. I was terrified!" As we talked, I found out that she had been feeling the same fight or flight that had consumed me now I was afraid for the guys still out there. Were they in any danger?

Cari and I sat in the chairs in our backyard. I wanted to be close to the woods in case the guys ran into any trouble with the way I had felt I knew that was a possibility.

As we sat facing the woods, we kept hearing footsteps and the heavy whoosh sound that we have related to their breathing. I was growing more and more concerned with the guys, being out there.

I heard a loud branch break to my right as I peered into the dark woods, it seemed as if two red eyes were looking at me! I blinked hard and looked again, yes! I could see them now! Were they moving?! They seemed much clearer, as I strained to focus on these eyes. I watched these eyes steadily coming closer through the woods; I stood up from my chair with my eyes glued to these, and I slowly started to walk backward. I turned on my flashlight and shined it in that direction. It seemed as if it started coming faster toward the light. By the look of the eyes, whatever this was, was very tall. "Cari," I said softly. "Cari"....She grabbed me by the arm breaking my stare we turned and made a run for the house. We could hear the whoosh behind us! We made it to the front door, shaking and breathing hard.

"What in the world?" Cari exclaimed!

"I have no clue what that was," I gasped. "But it was heading for us in a hurry!"

Cari and I stayed inside until we could get our nerves calmed down a bit. I kept thinking about what I had just seen. What had that been? Why was it coming toward us and not spooked by our flashlights? I needed to go back outside, so I could hear if the guys called out. I knew there was something in those woods with them, and that frightened me. Cari and I walked very slowly back into the yard. We were both proceeding with caution, we had no idea what was out here with us, and even if it was still here. We settled back into our chairs and waited. Every few seconds I am looking over my shoulder. The feeling of being watched was the strongest I have ever felt. We sat facing the woods and straining our ears for the slightest sound of the guys.

"Do you hear that?" Cari asked.

I strained to listen....footsteps; I could faintly hear the leaves crunching underneath the feet. The longer I listened, the closer they came.

"What is that?" I wondered aloud.

The steps were getting louder and faster. It sounded like something was on a mission. The walking was coming from the center of the woods and straight toward our chairs! One loud tree break in the middle of hearing these footsteps sent us both running for the house! I knocked over my chair, jumping up so quickly! Our guys did not snap that tree like that! Something once again was seeking out Cari and me! We made it back inside and this time, we were staying. What help would we be to them anyway if this thing was interested in us? Now I was afraid for the guys. Why didn't they just come back to the house now? I had not taken any walkie-talkies with us, as we were all together to start with. (Lesson learned here.) The cell phone! I grabbed the house phone to give Marty a call! I could tell him to head home now, and everything would be fine. My hands trembled as I dialed the number. I got his voicemail. Damn it! Next, I tried Chris's phone, It rang somewhere in the back part of the house. He had left it in his bedroom. Now I had no way to reach them. No way to warn them.

While we waited for them to come home, Cari and I were intermittently getting up and walking out to the gate to peer into the dark woods. Where were they? Two hours later, the guys come to the front door. They were talking to each other about their experience as they entered the dining room where Cari and I sat. You guys were gone forever, I said. What happened?

They all three sat down and started telling us of the night's events. After Cari and I had left them, they continued deeper into the woods. After a while, they started noticing footsteps on both sides of them. The walking noise always stayed just where their lights could not penetrate the dark. Each time they would stop to listen, the footsteps would stop too. This continued for quite a way into the woods. After they had got down to the swamp, they started to hear some wood knocks one was close by but the answering one was further down the swamp. They started doing a few knocks themselves and getting responses after a few minutes wait. They followed the knocks along the swamp, but never saw anything. Eventually, the woods fell silent, so they started back home.

As they neared the house, they were once again met by something walking close to them. They stopped to listen. They heard some very deep breathing. As they were trying to pinpoint exactly where it was coming from, they started hearing the all too familiar sound of a rock coming through the tree branches. The rock hit the ground just a couple of feet away with a loud thud. They knew they were no longer welcome and came on home.

After hearing their story, Cari and I told them what had happened to us. We could only speculate that the one that had been harassing us girls met them on their way home and threw the rock at them. What a night we had!

The five of us went out to check the woods the next day. The majority of the ground is covered with leaf litter, so it is almost impossible to find good tracks. We occasionally see large footprints, but they just are not good enough to photograph much less try to cast. We came across a few tree structures that I don't remember seeing before.

Therefore, it is quite possible something did this overnight. There was no more evidence to be found. Like most of our encounters, we all walked away with nothing more than our own feelings and experiences. I can say, though, It rather validates your experience to have someone with you that sees and hears the same thing!

A few nights ago, we decided to grill some chicken and steaks. Marty sat up the grill at our usual spot in the lower part of the yard. Being next to the tree line and in a slight hollow, it is much cooler down there than the rest of the yard. He started up the fire, and we were waiting for the coals to die down. I heard something hit the ground near the grill; it was a very light sound, so I assumed something had fallen from a tree. A few minutes later, the same thing happened. I got up from my chair and walked over to the tree line nearest the grill. It wasn't long until another hit the ground. I was watching this time, so I saw exactly where it fell, I walked over and picked up what turned out to be a very small rock. Now we know that didn't fall out of any tree. I went back to my chair and sat down watching the woods for any sign of movement.

As I sat back down, I noticed a different color in the trees that I had not seen earlier. I can't say if this is anything more than a change in the leaves. But it looked out of place to me, so I snapped a photo. (I have yet to check these.) Right after this, we heard a very loud tree knock come from our left. We had apparently been spotted. After this, our neighbor decided to do some late evening target practicing. The sounds of gunfire changed what we hoped to be an active night into a washout. We picked up our things and headed for the house. Maybe our trail cam will catch something later in the night.

Since I have had a couple of experiences that unnerved me. Or just flat out scared the pants off of me maybe more like it. I have started noticing that many people want to go out and look for Bigfoot. Just as I did, without truly researching this creature first. It is not all fun and games like I may have thought in the beginning. Is tracking a grizzly bear fun?
OK, It maybe for some people. But I don't see it that way. This is an undomesticated animal and it's unpredictable.

Are you ready to stand face to face with something you always considered a myth? Can you handle looking up at a creature that could quite possibly be eleven feet tall? I strongly advise you to ask yourself these questions before you go in search of this creature. And please, don't go alone. It really isn't safe for anyone to be out exploring the woods alone.

Now, on the other hand. If you are seeking that Bigfoot experience, get out there. You won't find that on the pages of a book or your TV screen. It's going to take endless hours prowling the woods. My advice would be to start where you know one has been spotted. For us, that was the easy part.

I hope you have enjoyed our Sasquatch encounters, let us know in the reviews/comments!

On the following pages, I have added some of our team's unedited experiences on our last overnight expedition here in our research area.

Brandon Hudgens

Saturday, May 3, 2014

Overnight Bigfoot Expedition (Training Grounds)

Toured the grounds and looked at the new structures that were created. Marty, Chris, and I went into the woods further to see if there was anything new. We found a few things to go back and look at.

That night Chris and I began our expedition on the north side of the woods around the "gifting block" and sat. We knew that Cari and Lisa would be near the house at the edge of the woods, and Marty, Jean, Laverne, and Michelle were further in on the Southside of the woods before you get to the fenced area. As the night began, Chris and I began to see lights flashing in the woods. We went to investigate what it could be but an approaching skunk stopped us. Being that they are not afraid and this one began to move straight toward us, we left that area immediately and moved back to our original position. We did discover that the lights were lightning bugs. As we sat, we began to hear movement behind us. This movement was heavier, and it sounded like a person walking. I told Chris that we should check it out and we began to move toward the team at the South end.

At first, I thought that someone was trying to play a trick on us, but being that you could not see a foot in front of your face, we ruled that out immediately. As we moved toward the team on the south end, we could see their flashlights aimed in the direction of where Chris and I heard movement. This tells me that they heard the same thing. As Chris and I moved closer, we saw something move. It was tall, brown, and had a round head. We only saw it for a moment because it stooped. We decided to keep the flashlight on it and move toward it as Chris shined his flashlight in front of us to see where we were going. At that time, we heard movement again. When I shined my light, we saw the same thing repeatedly it stooped and stopped moving. Chris and I decided to move right to where it stopped. When we got there, we saw nothing. Nothing moved again. I cannot explain how this happened. Something should have been there because it never made another noise.

I cannot say that we saw Bigfoot, but we saw something, and it cannot easily be explained.

Brandon Hudgens, CPI Founder/Director
Carolina Society for Paranormal Research and Investigation Inc (CSPRI Inc)

Laverne Zimmerman

May. 4, 2014

Last night walking through the woods with my
teammates who are teaching me how to search for
legends like BigFoot, while enjoying the adventure of
the research (checks off one more item from my
bucket list).

Our group of 10 researchers was camped out on 26
acres of private land in the foothills of the mountains.
We expected this to be an interesting night. This area
had already shown activity in the form of Tree
structures, wood knocks, whoops and rock clacks.
The first structure I saw through the haze of
flashlights during the wee hours of the morning was
magnificent. I have got to meet whatever it was that
has the strength and height and brains to design and
put this structure together, with no nails, glue,
ropes.....designed by the placement of the trees only
for the support! As we continued through the thick
underbrush and dense trees, we saw smaller ones
and ornate ones and plain ones built similarly to the
awesome giant one.

It was quiet in the woods as we all spread out looking for our own spot in the dark to wait patiently while listening for a movement and a sound. We heard someone yell, "Rocks are being thrown at us," then silence. We sensed something watching us, heard heavy footsteps behind us, in front of us and suddenly heard a heavy thud. What sounded, we discussed later, like a huge tree limb fall on the ground between Marty and me! It was too dark to see what it was so I asked Marty if he had made that noise. He didn't. We flipped our flashlight on and pointed it to the ground between us. Nothing. We heard it hit the ground right between us! Nothing. We heard walking between two other teammates and us. At the same time, they flashed their light toward us and we did the same toward them. Nothing. How can noise be made by nothing? We all heard it, felt it so close to us, but by the time we get our lights on it.... Nothing! We are not crazy and we are not easily fooled. Something was there with us, but was not one of us, but what?

That's what this expedition was about, and I wanted to learn as much as I could about Big Foot's footprints, structures, habits, sounds, size. What I have learned in our group is among hundreds of thousands, maybe millions of others all over this world searching for this same legend. He has been seen thousands of years ago in other countries, and just as likely glimpsed only a day or so ago in our own country by many others out there like us is searching.

As I lay here in our tent, contemplating what I had seen, felt, and heard.....suddenly... A scream. I heard a torturous scream like nothing I have ever heard that startled me, so I sat up quickly in my sleeping bag. The scream also woke my sister.
She sat straight up. Both of us holding our breath and listening. The second scream was horrible. I wanted to help. But where? How? Then the scream became a gurgle, then no more! Silence. Eerie silence! No sound at all! Deadly Silence! Then the mooing of a cow became the only sound of the night. At 3:00 am in the morning!

Finally settled down again, and I heard the soft snoring of my two tent mates. I was still restless because I felt or sensed something. I could see a shadow go by our tent, heard it walk around the tent several times and stop. Heard breathing that sounded like grunting, so I reached for my stun gun and iPhone. I got my iPhone turned toward the screened door opening of the tent and was prepared to either defend myself with the stun gun or take a picture of this creature with my iPhone. Seriously! I was focused and prepared. Then whatever it was walked away. The trail camera was pointed toward our tent. I am hoping it captured something. But whatever this is that is now stalking us can disappear as quickly as we can blink an eye. Now I can be counted among all the others who want to be one of the first to solve this age-old question of what or who is Big Foot. Does he come and go through a portal or does he live in the flesh in our today's world?

Not to be taken seriously by those who make fun of what others claim to have seen, just Doesn't bother me.

This is not about them anyway; it's about me, all about me and the others who believe we share this world and universe with more things we don't know about than those things we do know about! That's the way it is and the way it will always be. God gave us free will to search for answers for things we don't understand and have a healthy hankering to investigate and learn about.

Laverne Zimmerman Paranormal Investigator CSPRI, Inc
Researcher
CCC, Inc

BF Expedition Private Research Site 5-4-2014
Dennis W. Carroll. My Experience,

In my 40 plus year career, in the field of paranormal research and investigation, the area of cryptozoology has always been a favorite of mine. I remember way back in the year of 1971 when I came across a book on the Yeti (abominable snowman of the Himalayas) and an old movie which starred Peter Cushing (The Abominable Snowman), that my curiosity was aroused to the mystery of this creature and that of its North American cousin the Sasquatch (Bigfoot). I read and researched thousands of case histories and reports that covered any and everything about the so-called Cryptid creatures of this world; Cryptozoology opened up a completely new, fascinating area of the paranormal for me. I was already involved not only in Ghosts and demonology but ufology and earth anomalies as well. I've always been a folklorist and legend seeker who since the earliest days of my youth, has been captivated by the many mysteries of this world. The beings of cryptozoology have that tie to the mystery of the creatures that we know as monsters and monsters are known in almost every culture worldwide.

These denizens of the dark and unknown are not the only inhabitants of nightmares, but also they can be called something very close to a racial memory, embedded deep in the mind of mankind itself. When some friends of mine recently told me of some very strange activity that was happening very close to their home, me being me, no way was I going to turn down the opportunity to look deeper into these incidents. When my friend and colleague Brandon Hudgens and I had formed our paranormal team (Carolina Society for Paranormal Research and Investigation Inc) a few years earlier, we had been hoping that just such a case as this would come up. About ten years before this, I had looked into several reports of a strange hairy creature that had been sighted on a dirt road situated in the Broadway Lake area, on the outskirts of Anderson S C. (Which also involved several UFO reports), so I had some experience in very similar cases.

Also recently, I had checked out some sightings of
ABCs (Alien big cats) as well. Reports were coming
into us of strange structures in the woods and tree
knockings, along with very unusual night noises, in
the large tract of woods near the home of our friends,
then several large footprints were found in the woods,
one that we cast was 19 inches in length.

 This was and still is an excellent opportunity for
research, too good to pass up for any of us. So I
suggested to my friends that I would like to stake the
area out for a few hours of daytime observation.
Although I was to do this alone, I was also to keep in
constant contact via walkie-talkie with my friends
nearby. I set up a video camera on a tripod when I
established my area of observation. I was situated
very near to where the footprints were found, as I
figured this would be the perfect place for a possible
sighting. I kept a constant eye on the sky as the
clouds all day looked very threatening, and as the
summer heat was very oppressive, it was perfect
weather for thunderstorms. The spot I had was very
well hidden, and I settled in for a long time of
watching and waiting. As everything soon settled
down and returned to a relative state of normalcy....I
began to notice something very peculiar. Every hour
or so,

There would come a brief period of silence....even birds would quit singing. It immediately gave me the feeling as though something was circling my location, in the very thick brush around me. There was also that instinctive feeling of being constantly watched. My video camera at this time began to do some crazy things. I had my reliable handy-cam that day and it did some things it had never done before or has done since...on record it did only blank imaging, as if I were in extreme sunlight with it, which I wasn't. I was the whole time in the shade. It worked perfectly fine after I left those woods. Also, during the times of strange silence...I noticed a slight fluctuation in my compass. It was slight, however, and not dramatic. After about four hours, I noticed the sky getting darker and some distant thunder, so I knew it was time to leave. As I was packing my gear, I looked to my right, deep into the brush, I could see a patch of sunlight in a slight clearing, in the bushes probably twelve yards or so distant from me. It was then that I saw a very large shadow fall swiftly across this patch of sunlight. It was not a bird or even the size of a dog, but larger than the shadow of a man would be.

I immediately made for that clearing, but as I said, the brush there was very thick, and it took me some time to make it into that open space and of course, by then, there was nothing there to see. Thunder was getting louder; I knew I had very little time before the rain and the storm would break. I radioed my friends that I was on the way back in, and I left the woods and got back to their house just barely about the time the storm hit. The whole stakeout was very strange, and I felt most of the time that I was not alone out there in those woods. I see a definite future return to those woods for another possible stakeout, hopefully on the night of a very bright full moon. It Would I think, definitely yield some very interesting results...I'm looking forward to that...

Dennis W. Carroll CPI Founder/Assist. Director Head of InvestigationsDemonology Consultant

Carolina Society for Paranormal

Research and Investigation Inc. (CSPRI Inc)

Founder/Director American Institute

For Paranormal Research (AIPR)

Michelle Lynn Meyle Cooper
May 2014 Overnight Expedition

I want to explain to you all my experience that I had
in the woods one night. Now I have been in these
woods before in the daytime. I always look at the
ground for prints, as well as what the tree and ground
structure is. That alone can tell you a lot.
So that day, we set up a tent that three of us would
sleep in. That is three women sleeping in the woods.
We picked out a spot that overlooked the rest of the
woods. So we all meet back where we eat dinner as a
family and talk about what we were going to do. After
our gathering, we all broke up into small groups with
flashlights, cameras, and walkie talkies. We always
strive to be very professional! So we had three
different groups going out this time. We had two
groups of two people and one group of four. I was in
a group of four. Now it was dark and my group was to
go in the middle while the other two groups went out
on opposite sides. My group decided to sit down on a
big tree that had fallen. While we sat there, we could
hear something walking around the outside of where
everyone was.

It's hard to explain completely. It was like something with a heavy foot. When we would shine our flashlights, the direction that we heard the footsteps it would disappear. We also had a limb break right behind us, we cannot explain how
it happened. Late after we all came back, together, we all talked, and we all hear the same thing. The other group didn't know about the limb breaking behind us, but we also didn't know that they had a rock thrown at them either.

Well, after all of the talks, we left and went back to the tent to settle in for the night and to see if we could hear anything that was out of the ordinary. We did hear a cow moo on and off all night, which is usual. It was also a very quiet night meaning no owls, crickets or anything that night.

That is the end of my experience because I fell asleep…. I know that there is something out there.

Carolina Cryptid Crew Investigator.

Cari George
May 4 Overnight expedition

The team planned an all-night Sasquatch expedition. This was unusual, we usually hit the woods in the afternoon, or at dusk- but the team was ready for an adventure. The Carolina Cryptid Crew gathered for a dinner of grilled hot dogs, discussed our plans and excitement, double-checked equipment.
And teamed up for the night.

We were in for an adventure. After a group walk in the woods and a plan of action was decided on, we split up for the night. Because Melissa and I usually have luck together, we decided to keep that constant. Little did I know- the next time I saw my teammates, I would be a changed person. After grabbing our flashlights, walkie-talkies, and other gear, Melissa and I headed out to find the perfect spot to wait for the sounds to begin; we knew they would come first. It didn't take us long to find a large tree with not much debris near it.

We decided on this location so we could turn off our lights and still cut down on the noise we were making. Right after deciding on this location, we noticed a stick that I could barely wrap my hand around just stuck down into the ground. It was broke off about 6 feet up and was just stuck there, standing straight up. I knew then that we had found the right spot. This was a place a Bigfoot had been.

Not even two minutes later, we hear the sounds of heavy, deliberate footsteps coming our way. It was only a few steps, but unmistakable. If you have ever heard a Sasquatch coming towards you, the sound is unforgettable, and unlike anything else, you will ever hear. We couldn't see our hands in front of our faces, it was so dark. We tried to use the walkie-talkie to let the rest of the team know what we heard. Unfortunately, ours was dead. Melissa yells to a group not far away from us to let them know. They answered back and continued on their expedition. There is always comfort in knowing that someone else is aware when such a massive beast is so close. Melissa turns the flashlight on, and we were expecting to see a large hairy being in front of us.

There was nothing there, it must have been just out of the flashlight's range. Being the investigators we are, Melissa and I decided to walk towards the sound. After taking just two steps, a rock came crashing towards us. We heard it flying through the trees. It landed where we had been standing. Melissa and I spun around and even spilled some four-letter words. We could not tell if the rock had come from in the tree or behind the tree, but we knew three things. We knew that if we had not moved, we would have been hit. There was a Sasquatch in front of us and behind us, both very close.

Most importantly, we knew that we had to get out of there. Melissa and I flew out of the woods, I did not know our legs could carry us that fast. We raced back to command central, to get a new walkie-talkie and catch our breath. None of the walkie-talkies would work, and that should have been a sign. We let our hearts stop racing, discussed what had happened, and decided to go back out. We found a location close to where we were first and decided to stay there. Almost immediately after making the decision, we get a surprise. All of a sudden, there are footsteps all around us. We were surrounded. I could tell that she had the same thought as me.

Melissa said, "Let's get out of here." We high tailed it out of there and back to command central. When we finally stopped, we agreed we would stay put the rest of the night. This was only the beginning. From about 10 o'clock that night until about 2 the following morning, we kept watch at command central. The whole time, we could feel we were being watched. I wish it had only been the feeling though. The whole time, there was something large and bipedal walking just in the edge of the woods. Melissa and I were hearing the very distinct sounds of tree knocks, rock clacks, and even whoops. There were other sounds that we never heard before, including a strange breathy growl. Rocks were being thrown in our direction and hitting the metal roof of command central. We even heard a large animal urinating behind a shed in the edge of the woods.

From the pattern of sounds and the type of sounds, Melissa and I speculated that the creature wanted to come out of the forest very desperately. However, the light from the streetlamp gave us the advantage. The sounds continued until the other teams started coming back to command central. While the other teams were planning on going back out for the night, Melissa and I decided to call it a night.

Melissa and I spent a couple hours going over the
night. The more we discussed it, the more we realize
what really happened. We intended to hunt for
evidence of Bigfoot's existence but got a surprise.
Instead of being the hunter, we were being hunted.
I have had plenty of time to digest the events of that
night. While some of my theories on Bigfoot have
remained the same, many have changed.

 While I still have great respect for these magnificent
beings, the respect has shifted from being of
admiration to that of reverence with some fear mixed
in. I had never had a reason to fear these things. I
had always believed that if our intentions were good,
then we would be okay. However, now I realize that
there is more to it than that. I know we could have
been taken or killed that night. For some reason, we
were spared. I do believe these Sasquatches that
surrounded us intended to scare us, and may have
intended for much more. I still intend on participating
in expeditions, but my expectations have changed. I
do not believe that anything short of a body will ever
prove the existence of Sasquatch, and even then it is
questionable.

To be honest, I don't think this will ever happen and I don't think I want it to ever happen. The thought of seeing them hunted for sport or put in zoos breaks my heart. That being said, after my experience, I'm not sure it is possible to ever get a Sasquatch body. I will remember that night forever, and I will be analyzing it forever. I have so many questions that I'm not sure will ever be answered.

Epilogue.

We have since learned that this creature frequents our property early spring to late fall. As soon as the wild turkeys start to move about, we know that is has come back for another summer. The crickets and bullfrogs will soon go silent, a still will fall over the area, then faintly in the distance, we will hear that familiar knock. I know these creatures exist, and I have made it my quest to learn as much as I can about them.

I hope you have enjoyed our expeditions and experiences.

Thank you for reading—Melissa

Follow the Carolina Cryptid Crew.

https://www.facebook.com/carolinacryptid.crew

http://carolinacryptidcrew.blogspot.com

https://twitter.com/CarolinaCryptid

http://www.carolinacryptidcrew.com/

https://www.youtube.com/channel/UC28kET3-pXvDJMGHHT7C76A?view_as=public

If you enjoyed this book, please consider leaving a review.

Also, you might want to check out some of Melissa's other titles.

1. <u>Bigfoot Chronicles,</u> A true story

2. <u>Bigfoot Chronicles 2,</u> A true story

3. <u>Sasquatch, The Native Truth</u>. A true story

4. <u>Sasquatch, The Native Truth. Kecleh-Kudleh Mountain</u> A true story

5. <u>Sasquatch, The Native Truth. Ravens Return</u> A true story

6. <u>The True Haunting of a Paranormal Investigator</u>

7. <u>Dog Man,</u> A True Encounter

8. <u>Black-Eyed Kids. My Three Months of Hell</u>. A true story

9. <u>Family Ties</u>. Fiction

10. <u>Female Bigfoot Encounters</u>. True Stories

11. <u>Our Paranormal Reality, A True Haunting</u>. Book 1 <u>The Early Years</u>

12. <u>Our Paranormal Reality, A True Haunting</u>. Book 2 <u>The Investigation</u>

13. <u>Bigfoot, A New Reality</u>. A True Story

14. <u>The Birth of a Psychic with Telekinesis</u>. A True <u>Story</u>

15. <u>Lifting the Veil on All Things Paranormal, True</u> <u>Stories</u>

16. <u>Desolate Mountain, One woman's true story of</u> <u>survival</u>.

17. <u>The Watcher, A true story</u>.

18. <u>Bigfoot Found me. One man's true encounter with Bigfoot</u>.

19. <u>Goodbye. A true story of an Ouija board experience</u>

20. <u>Sasquatch Travels. Based on a true story</u>.

21 <u>Dream House</u>

22. <u>Breast Cancer, Faith, God & Home Free</u>

23. <u>Wood Bugger. One boy's true story of growing up with Bigfoot</u>

24. <u>The Doll</u>.

25. A Week in Bigfoot Territory.

Melissa's books can be found online at

Amazon

Barnes and Noble

Books a Million

Wal-Mart

Or ask for them

at your local

bookstore.

Follow Melissa on,

Her Blog;

http://www.melissageorge.net/

Facebook;

https://www.facebook.com/MelissaGeorgeParanor malAuthor/

Twitter;

https://twitter.com/AuthorMelissaG

Pinterest;

https://www.pinterest.com/melissa6144/

Instagram;

https://www.instagram.com/authormelissageorge/

Get sneak peeks on upcoming books. And enjoy book giveaways with every new release!

http://melissageorge.net/

About the Author.

Melissa was born and raised in a small town in upstate South Carolina. She first became a well-known Blogger and later decided to take her writing a step further. Her first book, My Paranormal Life, A True Haunting, started out as her own private journal of her family dealing with a dark entity. But it doesn't stop there, Melissa took it even further and let her experiences help her to co-found a paranormal team and a cryptid team. She enjoys being able to reach out and help others. She has made many new friends in both of these fields, which has also led her to help others to have their story told. Melissa realizes first hand that these people have a very passionate and unique story that needs to be told. In getting these compelling stories out to the public, she hopes it will help further research in both of these fields, and just maybe the individual that shares their story with her may find some closure to their own personal nightmare. Melissa feels honored to be able to bring you true stories of the unexplained.

If you have a story you would like to see published or just want someone to talk to. I promise you complete anonymity. Melissageorge143@gmail.com